The New Testament – Which Way In?

The New Testament – Which Way In?

Kenneth Grayston

DARTON·LONGMAN+TODD

First published in 2000 by
Darton, Longman and Todd Ltd
1 Spencer Court
140–142 Wandsworth High Street
London SW18 4JJ

© 2000 Kenneth Grayston

ISBN 0–232–52388–6

The right of Kenneth Grayston to be identified as the author
of this work has been asserted in accordance with the
Copyright, Designs and Patents Act 1988.

A catalogue record for this book is available from
the British Library.

Designed by Sandie Boccacci
Set in $9^1/_2$/$12^1/_4$pt Palatino by Intype London Ltd
Printed and bound in Great Britain by
Redwood Books, Trowbridge, Wiltshire

Contents

Acknowledgements

Of the many friends who have contributed to the making of this book, I specially wish to thank Christine Stones and the Revd Dr Neil Richardson for their comments and encouragement; my former university colleague Beverley Leonard for getting the script in fine readable order; and the publisher's editorial staff for accepting the book and applying their skills to see it through.

Why Did I Write This Book?

Because it seems that people are no longer familiar with the Bible. If they worship on Sundays they hear passages read and perhaps explained. But such passages are seldom part of their own familiar knowledge. The Bible Society recently discovered that 37 million adults in England and Wales own Bibles, though 65 per cent of them said they had not read anything from the Bible in the last year. That is scarcely surprising since watching television may now seem preferable to reading; and the Bible, even in modern translations, is a puzzling collection of ancient stories and religious responses. There are (I am told) bright American university students for whom the Bible is a book they have heard of but never read.

If that is so, then we are losing connection with our origins. Western civilisation was brought into being and developed by people speaking and writing in Hebrew, Greek and Latin. Hebrew poetry was being composed and perhaps written down in the twelfth century BCE. Hebrew is still a spoken and literary language. Literature in Greek which began with Homer, perhaps as early as 800 BCE, provides some of the noblest dramatic and philosophic writing of our culture. It is still used to provide medical terminology, and in its modern form is the everyday language of Greece. In the third century BCE the Latin language began to be widely important, producing a literary treasury of drama, poetry, rhetoric, satire, history, agriculture and law. In due course it became the standard European language for learning of all kinds, and only recently ceased to be the liturgical language of Roman Catholics. It still provides names in biology and astronomy. Our own English language (of the West Germanic type) has been greatly influenced by both Latin and Greek.

Finally, there is the Bible, the common possession of the Christian Church: the Old Testament written in Hebrew (and a small part in the related Aramaic language), the New Testament written in everyday Greek. From the fourth century CE, the Bible was most widely known in a Latin translation called the Vulgate (intended for the common people, the original meaning of 'vulgar').

Let me pause to explain CE and BCE. In Europe it has long been the convention to give the date of events as BC (that is, before the birth of Christ) or AD (Anno Domini (Latin), in the year of the Lord). Now, however, to avoid offending Jewish writers, it is more sensitive to write 'Before the Common Era' (BCE), that is, before there were any Christians; and 'Common Era' (CE), when both Jewish and Christian writers may be indicating historical dates.

But now back to my main theme. At the end of the sixteenth century and the beginning of the seventeenth, England produced its two noblest literary treasures: the plays and poems of Shakespeare and the Authorized Version of the Bible. Shakespeare displays high life and low life in English and Welsh history (once notably in Scottish history), in European experience (most frequently in the Mediterranean) and in the formative civilisations of Greece and Rome. In the historical plays, politically powerful clergy are often leading characters, sometimes balanced by inferior clergy and friars – though Shakespeare's awareness of Christian conviction should be sought in the character of his 'fools' (as in 'We are fools for Christ's sake', 1 Cor. 4:10) and in such plays as *The Merchant of Venice* which presents fundamental religious questions for Jews and Christians.

The so-called Authorized Version of 1611 was simply called 'The Holy Bible. Appointed to be read in Churches.' It was never otherwise officially 'authorised'. It was 'translated out of the original tongues: and with the former translations diligently compared and revised, by his majesty's special command' – so in the USA it is commonly called the King James Version. The translators made use, without acknowledgement, of existing translations. Sometimes they were mistaken and misguided, occasionally obscure. They lacked the much fuller information we now possess, and their language is now archaic and sometimes misleading. But their version, in wonderfully direct seventeenth-century English, was a huge success – so that to possess and read this Bible belonged unquestionably to the British way of life.

No longer so! But we cannot allow the foundations of our western culture to become a revered but unread world classic. It would be like draining the Mediterranean and turning it into a landfill site. Yet we cannot rescue the Bible from its present puzzled neglect simply by insisting that it is the foundation document of our Christian theology and morals. Since, in the New Testament, we have a bundle of writings, composed in a now distant period of Mediterranean history, we need to use the historical skills that have been developed, mainly in Europe, from the middle of the eighteenth century onwards. If by that means we can discover when and why the various New Testament writings were composed, we have taken the first step to bringing them to life again. We can begin to ask: If newly made Christians, facing a hostile world, needed to say that then, what in our situation must we say now?

The (Greek) New Testament is a varied collection of writings, not best served by their traditional names.

There are four gospels by anonymous authors (i.e., the familiar names were not attached to the original Greek copies). They describe the activities and teaching of Jesus in the final year or so of his life.

The author of the third gospel (Luke) also wrote a continuation volume giving an historical account (Acts of the Apostles, largely devoted to Peter and Paul) of the development of Christian communities in the eastern Mediterranean, from Jerusalem to Rome.

There are nine letters in Paul's name, sent to named Christian Churches; and four letters sent to named Christians.

There are two letters in Peter's name. One is a circular letter to a group of Churches in what is now mainland Turkey. The other, a general letter, includes most of the material of a short letter in the name of Jude.

There are three letters, written in the style of the Fourth Gospel (John), by an unnamed author – probably by the 'elder' mentioned in two of them. They deal with faith, morals and community problems.

There is a treatise (Hebrews) that seeks the significance of the crucifixion by reflecting on biblical instructions for Jewish sacrificial practice and imagery. Its final chapter provides pastoral advice for a Christian community connected in some way with Italy.

Finally, there are letters written by John to the seven Churches of Asia Minor, enclosed in an Apocalypse (modelled on the second half of the book of Daniel) which discloses the expected violent ending of the Roman Empire and the foundation of a new world.

In all, there are twenty-seven writings that have been authoritative Christian scriptures for about 1,600 years. Earlier, some of them were disputed, and other early Christian writings were preferred. In present-day scholarship a great number of ancient documents are used to open up the meaning of the New Testament writings. But my present intention is to offer a programme for reading the New

Testament as it is. It is not an anthology like Palgrave's *Golden Treasury* of the best songs and lyrical poems in the English language, where you dip in according to your mood and interests. The New Testament is a group of writings that belong to the origins of the Christian Church, and they are most profitably understood if they are put into their historical and social background. I am not providing a commentary – an explanation and discussion of each writing – though sometimes explanations will be needed. If I am successful, readers will begin to discover what sort of explanations they need and what sort of responses they can make to the biblical text.

It is therefore essential that you should read not only what I say about the Bible but the Bible itself. Please have a Bible at hand and look up the references mentioned and the passages under discussion. My intention is not that you should remember what I say but what the Bible now says to you.

You will notice that parts of the New Testament are lengthily treated, parts only briefly. In my judgement lengthy treatment is merited when some book either makes a decisive contribution to my historical presentation or is particularly difficult for modern readers. Shorter treatment is permissible when help is readily available or when you yourselves are well placed to discover what the book is about.

In my *display* of the Pastoral Epistles, I am indebted to James. D. Miller, *The Pastoral Epistles as Composite Documents* (Cambridge University Press, 1997, pp. 185–94).

1 The Whole New Testament

We should take the advice given to Alice in Wonderland: *Begin at the beginning and go on till you come to the end: then stop.* Where the beginning is has yet to be decided, but the first suggestion is that we should read the whole New Testament, not merely some parts of it. It is not right to pick out texts (without considering context, argument and circumstances) to support our understanding of Christianity or to throw at those who disagree with us.

It is worthwhile pressing that point. I can easily offer you a collection of odd or disturbing extracts.

Unless your righteousness exceeds that of the scribes and Pharisees, you will never enter the kingdom of heaven (Matt. 5:20). Must we all outdo their inflexible devotion to ritual and moral rules?

Whoever blasphemes against the Holy Spirit can never have forgiveness, but is guilty of an eternal sin (Mark 3:29). Must we really endure the anguish of conscientious Christians who do not know what blasphemy against the Holy Spirit is or whether they have committed it?

See, I have given you authority to tread on snakes and scorpions, and over all the power of the enemy; and nothing will hurt you (Luke 10:19). Does what Jesus said to the seventy apply to (some of) us, and can Christians claim immunity from harm?

You are from your father the devil, and you choose to do your father's desires. He was a murderer from the beginning and does not stand in the truth, because there is no truth in him (John 8:44). Words addressed by Jesus 'to the Jews who had believed on him'. Is that how Christians should regard Jesus' own people, then and now?

'Ananias . . . You did not lie to us but to God!' Now when Ananias heard these words, he fell down and died . . . After an interval . . . his wife came in, not knowing what had happened . . . Then Peter said to her . . . 'Look, the feet of those who have buried your husband are at the door . . .' Immediately she fell down at his feet and died. (Acts 5:1–10). Whose performance is more repulsive: Ananias and Sapphira's, or Peter's?

Let every person be subject to the governing authorities; for there is no authority except from God, and those authorities that exist have been instituted by God (Rom. 13:1). Did that mean Hitler in Germany and the territories he conquered? And Pol Pot in Cambodia?

When any of you has a grievance against another, do you dare to take it to court before the unrighteous, instead of taking it before the saints? (1 Cor. 6:1). That would make legal redress even more difficult and uncertain than it is now.

Such boasters are false apostles, deceitful workers, disguising themselves as apostles of Christ. And no wonder! Even Satan disguises himself as an angel of light (2 Cor. 11:13–14). That is how Paul vilified Christian apostles who disagreed with his work at Corinth. The temptation to follow him is sometimes great, but should we?

Now Hagar is Mount Sinai in Arabia and corresponds to the present Jerusalem, for she is in slavery with her children (Gal. 4:25). What that meant to Paul and his readers in Galatia is difficult enough. What force could it have had when Jerusalem was destroyed in 70 CE? Even more now when Jerusalem is at the heart of Middle East turmoil?

Just as the church is subject to Christ, so also ought wives to be, in everything, to their husbands (Eph. 5:24). A command that has long been offensive to women and seriously damaging to men who are thereby deprived of the discoverable benefits of an equal partnership in marriage.

Beware of the dogs, beware of the evil workers, beware of those who mutilate the flesh (Phil. 3:2). If we are thus encouraged to abuse religious opponents, something more subtle and discreditable could now be found.

If with Christ you died to the elemental spirits of the universe [or, *the rudiments of the world*], *why do you live as if you still belonged to the world? Why do you submit to regulations, 'Do not handle, Do not taste, Do not touch?'* (Col. 2:20–21). Leaving aside the translators' uncertainty about this passage, and the meaning of the 'regulations', how can it possibly be supposed that we no longer belong to this world?

The Jews who . . . displease God and oppose everyone . . . Thus they have constantly been filling up the measure of their sins; but God's wrath has overtaken them at last [or *completely* or *forever*] (1 Thess. 2:14–16). But that sounds like a discreditable misjudgement, contradicted later by Paul himself and by the distinctive and persisting contribution of the Jewish people to religion, literature, music and science – despite their endurance of long ill-treatment and enormous suffering.

Anyone unwilling to work should not eat (2 Thess. 3:10) – which sounds like a justification of the workhouse, contrary to *Blessed are you who are hungry now, for you will be filled* (Luke 6:21).

I permit no woman to teach or to have authority over a man; she is to keep silent (1 Tim. 2:12) – which would put paid to Elizabeth I, Queen Victoria and Elizabeth II.

It is impossible to restore again to repentance those who have once been enlightened . . . and then have fallen away (Heb. 6:4–6). If that is the rule, who would venture to pass judgement on an erring fellow Christian – knowing how easily we ourselves can err?

There is one lawgiver and judge who is able to save and to destroy. So who, then, are you to judge your neighbour? (James 4:12) – which makes the preceding Hebrews quotation very perplexing.

Slaves, accept the authority of your masters with all deference, not only those who are kind and gentle but also those who are harsh. For it is a credit to you if, being aware of God, you endure pain while suffering unjustly (1 Pet. 2:18–19). That may have consoled Christian slaves in an empire dependent on slavery, but it also weakened Christian opposition to enslavement – with consequences that are still being felt.

These people, however, are like irrational animals, mere creatures of instinct, born to be caught and killed. They slander what they do not understand, and when those creatures are destroyed, they also will be destroyed . . . And so it goes on for ten more verses, ending thus: *It has happened to them according to the true proverb 'The dog turns back to its own vomit'* (Prov. 26:11) and, *'The sow is washed only to wallow in the mud'* (2 Pet. 2:12–22). Bitter denunciation may be pleasurable, but it helps rather to increase anger than to promote truth.

We know that those who are born of God do not sin, but the one who was born of God protects them, and the evil one does not touch them (1 John 5:18). That at least opens the door to corporate self-deception.

Fallen, fallen is Babylon the great! 'Come out of her, my people, so that you do not take part in her sins, and so that you do not share in her plagues . . . Render to her as she herself has rendered, and repay her double for her deeds . . . so give her a like measure of torment and grief . . .' and so on (Rev. 18:1–8). Who can escape gloating or disclaim vengeance, but what prospect do they offer of a satisfactory future?

General readers will no doubt be familiar with some of those passages and the questions that go with them. But not everyone may have noticed that they can be found in all parts of the New Testament. Anyone who has taken a thorough academic course will recognise some of them, and will have considered the responses that can properly be made.

For example, some passages may be misunderstood unless they are recognised as part of the author's complex argument, like the remark in 1 John that those born of God do not sin. Or they refer to the unusual situation of a particular Church, like the advice in 2 Thessalonians that those who will not work shall not eat. The promise in Luke that nothing will hurt you reflects the anxieties of wandering evangelists in the earliest expansion of the Church. The story in Acts of Ananias and Sapphira, and in 1 Corinthians of Paul's shocked surprise that Christians are expecting pagan law suits to settle disputes between Christians – both of these show the Church's need for confidence in its own reputation. What is more, the Churches had to deal with converts who fell away and then wanted to return (hence in Hebrews no second repentance), to deal also with adherents who held destructive opinions and permissive morality, such as the false apostles in 2 Corinthians, the evil workers of Philippians, and the irrational animals of 2 Peter.

Several passages give expression to the Church's origin in Judaism (such as in Matthew the Christian need to exceed the devotion of scribes and Pharisees; or quite differently in Galatians where Paul feels free to offer a persuasive argument based on Hagar and Mount Sinai). There was growing separation between Christian and Jewish communities both before 70 CE when Jerusalem was destroyed (hence Paul's sharp words in 1 Thessalonians) and after the destruction (as in the savage words of John 8). Still other passages reflect the Church's need to protect its life and maintain its growth in the world of Romano-Greek society to which Christians had to conform. Hence the instruction in Romans that Christians, because of their religious convictions, must obey the authorities; in Ephesians that wives should obey their husbands; in 1 Timothy that women should have no authority over men – thus accepting the common Hellenistic social standards; and in 1 Peter slaves are to be submissive to their masters (a hundred years earlier the slave revolt let by Spartacus had devastated and plundered the whole of Italy). Even so, alongside this conformity, there are passages that defy the dominance of state and society and confidently expect 'the world as they knew it' to pass away and be replaced by something new. So in Colossians Christians do not belong to this world but are expecting a new one, and in Revelation are beginning to see the alarming signs of transformation.

Those remarks, that are intended to provoke second thoughts about disturbing New Testament passages, suggest that we should seldom read a single verse but at least a chapter, preferably reading, rereading, and memorising. Just as poetry cannot reveal its inward power until it has become part of our memory bank, so biblical passages are largely ineffective unless they are immediately available for illuminating or qualifying what we are now reading. It should also be becoming clear that we need to know about Christian origins in a Judaism already modified by Greek culture and about Christian separation from Judaism. We should take account of the Church's precarious situation in the Empire and the consequent temptations towards conflict or accommodation. Paul's letters show that each Church might have its own difficulties and advantages. We must get used to the discovery that the gospel writers were responding to the needs and discoveries of Christian evangelists in the Mediterranean world. They were not backward-looking chroniclers recording events exactly as they happened (even if that were possible), but they were providing supporting and persuasive information for the survival and spread of the Gospel.

From which it seems that readers of the New Testament need to know – or at least have some awareness of – the primitive Church's history and its previous background in Judaism. The importance of historical narrative is indicated by the two Lukan books, the gospel and the Acts of the Apostles. But important as they are, they are not sufficient: they begin too late and end too soon. The gospel begins in the days of King Herod of Judea (somewhat before 4 BCE) and Acts discreetly ends before Paul's death. Nothing is said about the destruction of Jerusalem in 70 CE – probably when Mark was written, after which Matthew, Luke and John were most likely composed. And there is nothing to inform modern readers how the Jewish people came to be as they were in the lifetime of Jesus: for that, some knowledge of the Old Testament is needed, but even more of the Apocrypha (for example, the Books of Maccabees). So Acts needs to be supplemented fore and aft. But that is not the only qualification of Lukan history. Every historian is his or her own spin-doctor, giving a rotation to the narrative as he or she tells it. For all the attractiveness of Luke's story-telling and its invaluable preservation of ancient tradition, Acts smooths out the conflicts that appear in Paul's letters – about which Luke seems to know nothing.

Without Acts it would be difficult to produce an historical account of early Christianity, but alongside Acts must be placed other narrative information, especially from Paul's letters. Information about first-century Judaism cannot be provided by the Old Testament since the latest book it contains (Daniel) was written in the second century BCE. Somewhat later information can be found in the Apocrypha: which are a dozen or so writings present in the Greek version, but not the Hebrew, of the Old Testament. ('Apocrypha' is Greek for things held hidden or out of sight.) They formed part of sacred scripture in the early Church and long afterwards, though since the Reformation they have been given a secondary, non-authoritative position by Protestants. There can be no objection to using them for historical information. Even more informative are the Dead Sea Scrolls and the Pseudepigrapha.

The Dead Sea Scrolls are writings produced by or belonging to a Jewish sectarian movement (until recently almost unknown) in the period 200 BCE to 70 CE. There are some interesting (but not revolutionary) parallels, in organisation and convictions, between them and early Jewish Christianity. Any serious student of the New

Testament will need to be well acquainted with the Scrolls now that they have been completely published and can be reliably interpreted. Such a student must also take account of the Pseudepigrapha (another Greek word, indicating writings by a contemporary author who offers them under an ancient symbolic name). From the first century and from just before or after, some twenty-five are now well known, and it is certain that some of them were known to the early Christians and used by them. The Epistle of Jude 14–15 quoted 1 Enoch 1:9; and there is a section of 1 Enoch (chapters 37–71, The Book of Parables) which uses the expression 'Son of Man' (common in the four gospels but nowhere else), and may have been written in the last quarter of the first century CE. If so, it has an important bearing on Jesus' use of that puzzling title – if indeed it was a 'title', rather than an ambiguous self-reference.

Something must also be said about rabbinic teachings. They began to appear in writing about 200 CE and no doubt preserved re-membered teaching from earlier times – though whether they reach back to the varied teaching before 70 CE (the destruction of Jerusalem, the Temple and its staff) or reflect the more restricted teaching of Pharisaic survivors intent on renewing Jewish community life is a matter for experts. The resulting collections, which include Mishnah and Talmud, come from scholarly debate lasting at least until the middle of the sixth century. Mishnah contains the scholarly adaptation of Jewish law for later times and changing circumstances, and it makes a substantial book. It is the first part of the Talmud (more like a multi-volume encyclopedia) which is the body of Jewish civil and ceremonial law and legend. With caution they can help to understand the New Testament, but no one can assume that a particular saying is 'standard Jewish teaching'. Study of rabbinics is a speciality, but anyone might read with profit a section of the Mishnah called Aboth ('The Fathers') which is a selection of maxims on conduct and sayings in praise of the Law handed down in the names of sixty teachers who lived from 300 BCE to 200 CE.

It will be obvious that only professional students can be expected to be on familiar terms with so great and varied a body of material. They should certainly read some of it (not simply rely on what textbooks say about it) and use it to inform the people they will teach, in schools, colleges and congregations. But general readers need not be deprived of contact with the larger world. For example, C. K. Barrett has edited, with introduction and notes, a book called *The New Testament Background: Selected Documents* (revised edition: SPCK

1978). It provides short extracts that deal with the Roman Empire, the evidence of informal writings and formal inscriptions, the writings of philosophers and poets, samples of private religions of salvation, accounts of Jewish history and specimens of rabbinic literature, excerpts from the Dead Sea Scrolls, the Jewish philosopher Philo and the Jewish historian Josephus, selections from the Septuagint (the Greek translation of the Hebrew Bible) and the Targum (the translation of the Old Testament when, as in Jesus' day, Aramaic had become the common language of the people), and finally various examples of apocalyptic (a Greek word meaning the disclosure of secrets, particularly speculation about the forthcoming transformation of the present world as we know it). Even that selective list of contents suggests that modern readers of the New Testament are invited to make an imaginative and sympathetic journey into a different world.

But I can easily suppose some readers becoming impatient, in different ways. So let me return to my list of extracts. When the offensiveness of some of them strikes home – which may happen to believers as well as to non-believers – the response may be, 'Disgraceful – they should be denounced or ignored'. But they cannot be ignored: they were written by the same kind of people who produced the acceptable passages. And for non-believers there is much else in the New Testament that offends readers or invites derision. In contrast, conservative Christians might in effect say, 'It's in the Bible. Therefore it's true and obligatory. You must either find a more temperate understanding, or accept it as it is.' To which the reply must be, that it may have been true enough for the people who wrote it and obligatory for their time, but their time is not our time. I strongly suspect that the refusal to admit that we live in a different world implies that God has achieved none of his intentions in 2,000 years – which might be blasphemy against the Holy Spirit, for which there is no forgiveness so long as the refusal is maintained.

Other readers, however, might make an opposite response. If, as you explain (they may say), these disturbing passages may be attributed to the particular conditions of earlier generations, they are no concern of ours. They are therefore irrelevant to us. But if that line is taken, a great deal of the New Testament can be dismissed as irrelevant to us. All the miracles can perhaps be abandoned because they were recorded in a pre-scientific age. Most of the parables can go because peasant agriculture has largely disappeared – and so on. Or could we leave well alone and accept the New Testament as it is, but treat it like a famous relic of the ancient world such as the

Meditations of the Emperor Marcus Aurelius or the moral and historical writings of Plutarch, such as (in our own tradition) the heroic poem *Beowulf* or Chaucer's *Canterbury Tales*? From such as these we can receive stirring thoughts and shrewd advice: so perhaps from the New Testament. And that is how many people treat it. But in Christian tradition the New Testament points to a person, his actions and their consequences that provide the definitive relation between God and human beings in their historical existence.

That reference to 'historical existence' is essential. The Christian religion is not about the timeless relation between divinity and humanity but about the day-by-day relation between human beings (constantly responding to the changes in themselves, their families, social groups, and their prospects) and the divine wisdom and knowledge that is directing an unstable and still-changing world to its final state – whatever that may be.

So then, when in the New Testament we come across instructions to Christians and examples of their behaviour, we cannot necessarily transfer their rules and their obedience to ourselves. We must first say, 'What was their problem and how did they solve it?' Then, 'Is our problem like theirs and can we solve it in a similar way?' Or, 'With equal fidelity, how do we solve our own problem which is quite unlike theirs?'

We go to the New Testament because, according to the Christian experience of 2,000 years, it can be guaranteed to produce an encounter with God. It does not provide ready-made rules to obey; and to some readers that will be distressing. But, as Paul insisted, salvation is by faith, not by carrying out rules.

The encounter with God is more likely to occur if we can free ourselves from western literalism, from the naïve and stubborn assumption that nothing in the New Testament can be true unless it is literally true. We are reading literature that originated in the eastern Mediterranean where imaginative associations are as instructive as prosaic literalness, where also the responses of persons in community (rather than western individualism) are taken for granted. Let me give an example.

John 4:46–54 tells the extraordinary story of how Jesus, at a distance of about twenty-five kilometres, restored to life a royal official's son who had been at the point of death. But the tart remark of Jesus in verse 48 discourages us from marvelling at a miracle. In fact, there are no 'miracles' in John's gospel, but plenty of 'signs' – remarkable events that point beyond themselves to something more significant.

In this instance, what more significant matter is in mind? Well, notice that this is the second sign that Jesus performed in Cana in Galilee; the first was the Cana wedding feast in 2:1–11. There are plenty of 'signs' in the gospel, but only these two are numbered – so they belong together and are significantly related. Let us stay for a while with the wedding feast where water became wine. If we are Greek readers we recall the familiar generosity of the god Dionysus; but as Jewish readers we remember Israel as God's unfaithful wife who finally says, 'I shall go back to my husband again, for I was better off than I am now'. To which God ruefully says, 'She does not know that it was I who gave her the grain, the new wine, and fresh oil, I who lavished on her silver and gold' (Hos. 2:7–8). And so at Cana, is not water 'used for Jewish rites of purification' transformed into superabundant wine of rejoicing? Does not the whole story imply that a movement beginning in rural Galilee could be expected to restore the Jewish people to God in a repaired relation? Though it has to be noted that Jesus' mother was there – and she appears again when Jesus was hanging on the cross (19:26).

What more then is indicated by the second sign? Not now the general problem of repairing the marriage of the Jewish people to God, but a major obstacle to that restoration: the political government of Galilee. Under Roman sovereignty, Galilee was governed by the half-Jewish, half-Edomite Herod Antipas. Everybody knew about his unsavoury marriage and his killing of John the Baptist (Mark 6:17–28). His official title was Tetrarch (a petty dependent prince), though he was popularly called king (Mark 6:14) – and the father in John's story was 'an officer in the royal service'. Perhaps a Jew, perhaps a Gentile. If a Jew, then his son would be his likely successor. His son's death would perhaps ruin the whole household. Would Jesus rescue the son, the household and this official's service of a corrupt but effective ruler, this courtesy 'king'? Jesus keeps his distance – the distance has imaginative significance – restores the son to health, and the whole family become believers. That means followers of Jesus, to whom Pilate later says 'So you are a king?' (John 18:37). But perhaps the official was a Gentile (like the similar centurion in Matthew 8:5–13 and Luke 7:1–10). If so, this anticipates the Gentiles of Passover who said 'Sir, we wish to see Jesus' (John 12:21). One way or another, is this not another movement beginning in rural Galilee that may change the political governance of the people?

That example allows the reader to consider community relations, expects the reader to make appropriate cross-links with other references, and encourages an imaginative exploration of an apparently limited episode.

To demonstrate that these proposals are not merely my personal suggestions, we may take one more example from Paul: his encouragement and warnings in 1 Corinthians 10:1–13. In this epistle, baptism and the Lord's Supper are prominent precisely because they have become divisive. Being baptised by this or that evangelist gives status and security (1 Cor. 1:13–17); the Lord's Supper becomes an opportunity for the well-to-do to have a party, sharply divided from the poorer members (1 Cor. 11:17–22). But that will not do, for the Christian community is not just another gathering of people with a private religion. It is a body of people who knowingly stand at the end of one age and expect a new age to replace it (v. 11). Therefore they can look back to the formative experience of their ancestors, when the age of Egyptian slavery ended and the age of liberation began. And they can learn from their ancestors – who can benefit not only Jewish Christians but Gentile Christians too – that liberation has its problems as much as slavery. The ancient stories of Israel's release from Egypt (Exod. 13 – 14) were written down for our instruction and warning for they bore the *impress* of divine activity. (In verses 6 and 11 Paul says they were *types* and happened *typically*; 'typos' is Greek for 'impression'.) So the fleeing Israelites, under the cloud of divine protection, safely passed through the sea that separated slavery and freedom. Thus were they wholly dependent on Moses, as Christians by baptism are wholly dependent on the leadership of Christ. Even more, they were fed and watered by supernaturally provided food and drink. Paul is referring to the manna and to water from the rock in Exodus 16 – 17. His remark that the rock accompanied their travels is a preacher's gesture, making use of a familiar expression of his day: it is found in the *Biblical Antiquities* of an unknown author (called Pseudo-philo, because formerly ascribed – wrongly – to Philo of Alexandria). The book, which imaginatively retells Israel's history from Adam to David, was probably written in the time of Jesus. The real Philo, writing in the first half of the century, said that 'the flinty rock is the Wisdom of God, which he marked off highest and chiefest from his powers, and from which he satisfies the thirsty souls that love God. And when they have been given water to drink, they are filled with the manna.' Since Paul had already said that God had made Jesus Christ our wisdom (1 Cor. 1:30) it is not surprising that he now says that the 'rock was Christ'. His intention was to draw a parallel between the Israelites with their kind of baptism and heavenly food on the one hand and, on the other hand, the Corinthian Christians with their baptism and their supper of bread and wine – both parties behaving badly. From verses 8 to 11 it looks as if some Corinthian Christians imagined that the journey into freedom allowed the liberties of ecstatic pagan religion, of sexual opportunities, and of irreverence towards God. What Paul does is to belabour them with an imaginative understanding of Israel's formative exodus. He ends with pastoral encouragement: when the test comes, a way out will be provided. But he implies that nothing they or he can do will prevent the test. In other words, we must not expect God to give special protection to his own when others are in trouble and suffering. What we, his own, must do is 'not to set our desires on evil things' (v. 6). We are not offered automatic prohibitions or taboos, but we must make genuine moral choices.

These two examples allow the Spirit to suggest an interpretation for us now of writings that (in Christian conviction) the Spirit prompted long ago. They also indicate what kind of knowledge must be brought to bear: obviously, familiarity with John's gospel and 1 Corinthians – and knowledge of the Old Testament. A commentary should provide some necessary awareness of Galilean topography and politics, and some useful acquaintance with the Jewish writings of Philo and with Greek attitudes to Dionysus. And the willingness to understand why in verses 3–4 the food, drink and rock are translated as 'supernatural' in the Revised English Bible (REB) but 'spiritual' in the New Revised Standard Version (NRSV); and why in verses 6 and 11 the NRSV has 'examples' but the REB has 'warnings' and 'symbolic'.

2 Reading the Original and Translations

That brings me at once to the next thing that must be said about reading the New Testament.

Since it was written in Greek it ought to be read in Greek. But that is easier said than done. Not that New Testament Greek is a difficult language – a good deal easier than English. Take for example our use of *may* and *might* (the second of which is pronounced as if it were written 'mite'). 'May I come to see you?' asks permission; and 'Might I come to see you?' asks permission deferentially. 'You might have come to see me' implies that they ought to but did not come. 'They may come to see us' suggests possibility. 'They might come to see us' suggests less confident possibility. If the direct statement 'We may come to see you on Tuesday' is put into reported speech, it becomes 'They said that they might come to see us on Tuesday'. And then comes the trap into which many now fall: 'If they had not left the country, they might have come to see us on Tuesday' – which clearly means that they could not and did not. But many baffled English-speakers say 'they may have come', implying the possibility that they did come (although they had left the country) – which is ridiculous. It is equally ridiculous that 'may' is also the name of a month and of hawthorn blossom; that 'might' means great strength, and that the same-sounding word when written 'mite' means a small arachnid, or coin, or person.

Anyone who is clever enough to learn the English language and then speak or write it understandably is surely not to be baffled by New Testament Greek. But the point of my illustration is not only to tease English-speakers but also to suggest that most languages have subtleties that come naturally to the native speaker but must be learned and recognised by others.

Translation is not looking up words in a dictionary and then substituting whatever English word corresponds to the Greek. It is discovering how to express the Greek writer's intention in an English that is constantly changing. And the Greek writer's intention cannot simply be read off the page but must be discerned by familiarity with an adequate sample of other Greek writings of that period. They include the Old Testament in Greek which was itself a translation from Hebrew and Aramaic – pointing therefore to acquaintance with those languages, at least to the way in which they work.

But, many will say, why worry about ancient languages when satisfactory translations are readily available? Why not go back to the Authorized Version? The Authorized (or King James) Version is usually vigorous, often beautiful, always archaic, and sometimes wrong. It is wrong where the translators lacked our modern knowledge of manuscripts and language. That is why there are many modern translations – so numerous, in fact, as to create a problem of choice. Since 1952 there have been two new English translations of the New Testament every three years. Some are revisions, some are for particular readers, some are to promote special theological convictions. Most recently there have been determined attempts to use inclusive language (so that women readers are not ignored when the biblical writers were clearly referring to both men and women). Further still, translators are pressed to use expressions sensitive to the responses of disadvantaged readers. Thus, not 'the blind regain their sight', but 'people who are blind regain their sight' – because they are primarily people, secondarily blind people. This seems to have been an American initiative and is pressed most strongly when the biblical text, translated incautiously, seems to be hostile to all Jews.

Many translations are now available and (because publishing is expensive) they are being pushed with marketing skills. Only an expert who has made careful comparisons can judge whether they are reliable and readable. From what such an expert tells me, I offer you seven recent translations, beginning with the information that there are two types of translation.

Type 1 reproduces, more or less effectively, the wording and manner of speaking of the Greek. That has benefits for students who need help with their Greek or who want to get close to the actual manner in which a biblical writer expressed his thoughts. In this Type there is the New Revised Standard Version (NRSV 1989), improving on the pioneering Revised Standard Version (RSV) (1946), which itself rewrote the American Standard Version which was an American adaptation of the Revised Version (1881). Also in Type 1 is the New

International Version (NIV) which is conservative evangelical in intention.

Type 2, now more favoured, translates statements in the Greek into a corresponding manner of speech in modern English. That is sensible if modern readers are to hear the Bible, not in a special biblical English but in their own speech – though there are varieties of modern English and the New Testament may refer to matters that are little known in modern experience. There are five worthy translations of this kind. Taking them in order of date, there is first the New Jerusalem Bible (NJB 1989, revising the Jerusalem Bible of 1966), an elegant Catholic translation, accompanied by fairly extensive explanatory and theological notes. Nowadays notes are often necessary and welcome, but some of these are contentious. Then there is the Revised English Bible (REB 1989), a revision of the New English Bible (NEB 1961) and sponsored by a joint committee of the British Churches. It presumes a fairly good level of education. The Good News Bible (GNB, second edition 1994), also known as Today's English Version, was designed for those who have English as a second language. Some find it most friendly for general use. The Contemporary English Version (CEV 1995) is written in natural idiomatic English for people not reading the Bible, but *hearing* it read. It is the kind of paraphrase that would properly be said in the classroom or pulpit. Finally, there is the New Living Translation (NLT 1996), a conservative evangelical paraphrase, concerned to overcome historical and cultural barriers.

In what follows I shall normally quote from the NRSV or REB.

Granted that such modern versions, backed by great learning and translation skills, are available, reading them is not the same as engaging with the scriptures in their original languages. Let me offer a few examples.

Matthew 7:1
'Do not judge, so that you may not be judged.' (NRSV)
'Do not judge, and you will not be judged.' (REB)

The Greek verb *krino* (from which we get 'critic') can mean distinguish, consider, decide, pass judgement, or condemn. The prohibition is in the *present* grammatical form, and it implies 'Do not go on condemning' – in order that you may not be condemned. By whom? Presumably by God – to avoid frequent and commonplace naming of God, Jewish speakers often used a *passive* verb, and knew that their hearers would understand. So what Matthew wrote means: 'Stop being censorious, that God may not condemn you.'

Matthew 23:23
'Woe unto you, scribes and Pharisees, hypocrites!
For you tithe mint, dill and cummin, and have neglected the
weightier matters of the law: justice and mercy and faith.' (NRSV)

'Alas for you, scribes and Pharisees, hypocrites!
You pay tithes of mint and dill and cummin; but you
have overlooked the weightier demands of the law – justice,
mercy, and good faith.' (REB)

This is part of a ferocious denunciation by Jesus of scribes and Pharisees. The damaging word is 'hypocrites'. According to the *New Oxford
Dictionary of English* hypocrisy is the practice of claiming to have
higher standards or beliefs than is the case. To most of us it means
knowingly pretending to approve and support what you do not. Is
that what Jesus was saying about learned experts in the Law and
influential, devout lay men? In Greek a *hupokrites* is a play actor,
someone who plays a part or pretends. More than a century and a
half before Jesus, the tyrant Antiochus was having the aged Jewish
leader Eleazar tortured, trying to make him eat swine's flesh – against
the prohibition of the Mosaic Law. Out of pity for him, some of his
torturers said, 'We will set before you some cooked meat; save yourself by *pretending* to eat pork.' Eleazar cried out, 'Never may we,
children of Abraham, think so basely that out of cowardice we feign
a role (hypocritise) unbecoming to us' (4 Macc. 6:12–17). Jesus was
not accusing the scribes and Pharisees of pretending to be devout but
of making a public performance of their devotion, of being public
good examples even in the tiniest matter of honouring God when
much more serious needs of God's people needed attention.

2 Timothy 3:16
All scripture is inspired by God and is useful . . .

or

Every scripture inspired by God is also useful . . . for teaching, for
reproof, for correction, and for training in righteousness. (NRSV)

All inspired scripture has its use for teaching the truth and
refuting error, or for reformation of manners and discipline in
right living. (REB)

Those translations are attempts to make sense of a defective Greek
sentence which lacks a verb and goes like this:

$$\left.\begin{array}{l} \text{Every} \\ \text{All} \end{array}\right\} \text{ writing inbreathed by God} \left\{\begin{array}{l} \text{and} \\ \text{also} \end{array}\right\} \text{ useful ... etc.}$$

(i) 'Writing' translates *graphe*. The author is not referring to writing in general but to the 'sacred writings' (*hiera grammata*) with which Timothy has been familiar from childhood (v. 15). He was a Jewish boy and had early learnt the Mosaic Law, perhaps beginning with Leviticus. The Pastoral Epistles make little reference to Hebrew scripture. The Second Letter of Timothy (2:19) quotes five words from the Greek of Numbers 16:5. The First Letter of Timothy (5:18) quotes the *graphe* of Deuteronomy 25:4 to justify double payment for good church leaders; and then requires any charge against an elder to be supported by two or three witnesses – the standard Mosaic rule (Deut. 17:6). Titus has nothing. Of course, by the time these epistles were composed, the Temple was destroyed and the practice of the liturgical commandments had become impossible. In the undoubtedly Pauline writings *graphe* six times refers to a particular passage, once to scripture as a whole.

(ii) 'Inbreathed by God' renders *theo-pneustos* (*theos*, God, and *pneustos* – from which we get pneumatic – comes from *pneo* which describes the wind blowing or people breathing). It is a very uncommon word, known elsewhere only in pagan sources, for example the Greek philosopher and biographer Plutarch, contemporary with the Pastoral Epistles.

(iii) What the writer is saying is surely this: even if a great deal of the sacred writings is now apparently dead, God can breathe life into them so that they become useful in some way other than their original intention. 'Useful' is rather a key word in these epistles (1 Tim. 4:8; Titus 3:8). In this verse which appears to be grammatically defective the author is scarcely making a profound statement about the inspiration of scripture – rather he is jotting down a note that even an ancient law in Deuteronomy can prompt a teaching programme for his Christian community.

These three examples of translation may by chance have indicated how these two versions differ. The NRSV cautiously sits close to the Greek and is a little old-fashioned in its language. The REB hopes to make modern sense by sometimes taking modest liberties with the Greek.

But never forget that for Christians the word of God is in Hellenistic Greek, not in any other language – for even the Jewish scriptures are referred to in a Greek version. It is indeed true that ancient biblical Hebrew and Palestinian Aramaic are often necessary guides to the interpretation of biblical Greek; but it is one of the irremovable consequences of the incarnation that the word of God was written down in Greek.

3 Begin at the Beginning

So we come at last to beginning at the beginning. Page one of the New Testament offers the gospel according to Matthew, with the genealogy, birth and infancy of Jesus. Since the name of Jesus appears in every book of the New Testament, and since the Christian religion is entirely bound up with him, that seems a suitable beginning. But if you first read Matthew and then move on to Mark you will be disappointed. For in Matthew you have already encountered almost everything in Mark, and a great deal of Matthew has been left out. If you now turn to Luke you will find it fuller than Mark but considerably different from Matthew – though Matthew, Mark and Luke are obviously telling the same basic story in similar ways, with much overlapping material. The writers have worked out their own tapestries to display a common design; but when we look for that design in John's gospel we are presented with something like a Persian carpet. Each gospel is a carefully contrived work of narrative art, and we must resist the temptation to amalgamate them into a single, more-or-less coherent story. In the middle of the second century, an Assyrian Christian called Tatian made an edition of the four gospels in a continuous narrative. With the Greek name Diatessaron ('by means of four') it became the standard gospel in Syriac-speaking churches till the fifth century. Apart from that episode, Christian Churches have maintained the separate gospels, though popular piety has sometimes favoured one rather than another, or allowed them to lapse into a muddled Diatessaron attached to the Christian Year.

Let us try a different approach. In my Greek Testament the New Testament occupies 680 pages. The letters attached to Paul's name provide 154 pages, only exceeded by the 186 pages of Luke–Acts. And in Acts, the first quarter is given to Peter and Stephen, the second quarter to Paul and Peter, and the final half to Paul. Clearly the mission and theological convictions of Paul dominate the New

Testament, even though the Johaninne writings (gospel, epistles and – surprisingly enough – Revelation) contribute 135 pages. The additional support for Peter is only 20 pages (1 Peter, which is similar to a Pauline letter, 2 Peter and Jude). Because Acts is much interested in Paul, probably Luke's gospel was attached in some way to the Pauline mission to Gentiles. Matthew's gospel, with its strong devotion to the Mosaic Law, is obviously written for a Jewish-Christian community. The Epistle of James writes Christian ethics in the Jewish wisdom tradition, and Hebrews develops a theology of the cross by drawing on Jewish sacrificial imagery. If Matthew, James and Hebrews are loosely put together, they require 122 pages. There remains Mark with 62 pages.

Paul	154 pages
Luke–Acts	186
Peter and Jude	20
Matthew, James, Hebrews	122
Mark	62
Johannine writings	135

It is a slightly odd collection, written over a period of fifty-five years (50–105 CE), and no more than a selection of early Christian writings. For example, the famous Codex Sinaiticus of the late fourth century included the whole of the New Testament, as well as the Epistle of Barnabas (probably written between 70 and 100 CE) and part of the Shepherd of Hermas (second century). In recent times many early Christian writings have been discovered or reassessed, some of them composed by non-mainstream writers (in a perverse and heretical manner). There are now insistent demands from some learned authorities that the interpretation of primitive Christianity should attach authority to these extra-biblical documents. But for the present, Christians have enough on their hands if they stay with the canonical New Testament.

If the canonical writings were written during about fifty-five years, can they be set out in time sequence? What, for example, is our earliest written evidence that Jesus died and was raised from the dead? Not the gospels but 1 Thessalonians. That he was crucified and raised? Not the gospels but 1 Corinthians. The business of producing a chronology of the New Testament is a technical matter, allowing for much disagreement. It depends on discovering and assessing indications within the writings themselves and putting them alongside a competent knowledge of eastern Mediterranean affairs. For example, the famine in the reign of Claudius (Acts 11:28); the year of Sergius Paulus' proconsulship in Cyprus (13:7); Claudius' expulsion of Jews from Rome (18:2); Gallio's proconsulship in Achaia (18:12); and the year when Porcius Festus succeeded Felix (24:27). All of which things happened before the destruction of Jerusalem in 70 CE. With a good deal of give and take it is possible to relate Paul's activities to the scheme of Acts, at the end of which Paul is left a prisoner in Rome for two years, probably 56–58 CE. Thereafter all is speculation, though we may perhaps add the tradition found in the *Ecclesiastical History* of the third-century Eusebius (to which there is no rival tradition) that Paul was martyred in Rome in the Neronian persecution of 67.

Before rewriting the contents list of the New Testament in probable chronological order (where I am in close agreement with the encyclopaedic work of Udo Schnelle, *The History and Theology of the New Testament Writings*, 1998), let me warn you that some writings will appear as not written by the author whose name they bear. Some readers find that view shocking, and seek to overturn it. To me it seems to matter very little, because the respect we give to these writings depends on the matter they contain rather than on the reputed author. (See my note on Pseudonymity on p. 117.)

Here then are the Pauline letters, written between 50 and 60 CE.

1 and 2 Thessalonians
1 and 2 Corinthians
Galatians
Romans
    (Paul arrives in Rome in 56 and stays at least till 58.)
Philippians
Philemon
Colossians – perhaps indirectly Pauline (58–60).

Everything else in the New Testament was written either in immediate relation to the fall of Jerusalem in 70 or as a consequence of that catastrophe. The Temple had been destroyed, sacrificial worship was no longer possible, the Sadducean priesthood had disappeared and Jerusalem could no longer be the sacred city of the Jews and the mother city of Christians. With the approval of the Romans, the Pharisaic teacher Yohanan ben Zakkai set up his centre (at a town near the coast, west of Jerusalem, the modern Yavne) to work out his conviction that only by the strictest performance of the Law could recovery be possible for sinful Israel. In that same period, the various

Jewish–Christian, Gentile–Christian components of the Church began to write down and formulate their traditions and to come to terms with the changed – and possibly still changing – situation.

Here then are the approximate periods in which the Christian writings were probably composed.

65–70	Mark's gospel
70–90	Luke's gospel and Acts
	Hebrews
80–100	Matthew's gospel
	James
	Ephesians
90–95	1 Peter
	Revelation
90–100	John's gospel and epistles
100	Pastoral Epistles
	Jude
105	2 Peter

From all this it must appear to Christians that the first hundred years after the birth of Christ were packed with outstanding events and the years from 50 to 100 with essential writings.

When we begin at the beginning, do we mean the events or the writings? If we mean the events, then Mark gives us John the Baptist proclaiming in the wilderness, Luke and Matthew give us diverse birth stories, and John takes us to the beginning of creation. If we ask Paul, he will say Abraham or Adam or (like Peter) the resurrection. It is less confusing to begin with the writings.

4 The Letters of Paul

It may be helpful to begin with a brief account of Paul's life. The fuller biographical information is in Acts, but there are first-hand references in Galatians 1:13 – 2:15 and Philippians 3:5–6.

He was born and brought up in a devout Jewish family in the learned, Hellenistic city of Tarsus (near the coast in the extreme south-east of Asia Minor). Whatever Paul did, he did with resolution and vigour. As a devoted Pharisaic exponent of Jewish tradition he persecuted the new Christian movement – until God revealed his Son to him (i.e., he converted from Pharisaic Jew to Christian Jew) with responsibility for proclaiming him to non-Jews. He did that for three years in Arabia with headquarters in Damascus. Then, after a brief informatory visit to Christian leaders in Jerusalem, he continued for fourteen years as an independent evangelist in his home territory of Asia Minor. In the next phase, the two enterprises (one promoted from Jerusalem by Peter and the apostles, the other promoted in Asia Minor and Antioch by Paul and his colleagues) were first co-ordinated at a Jerusalem consultation, and then broken apart by a dispute between Paul and Peter in Antioch. Thereafter Paul vigorously promoted his Gentile mission in Asia Minor, usually with Ephesus as headquarters. He established Churches in midland Galatia, then across the sea in northern Greece (Thessalonica, Philippi) and the south (Corinth). From the Churches so established he collected aid to help and propitiate Jewish Christians in Jerusalem, with the intention of then visiting the existing Christians in Rome and going on to evangelise Spain. But it went wrong. Paul was taken as an accused prisoner to Rome where he died or was put to death.

It is a matter of the greatest consequence that the earliest information we have about Christianity is in the form of letters. Paul adopted and developed the standard Greek style of letter-writing. The *writing* of a letter indicates the need to communicate. The author has been willing to arrange his thoughts, write them down, and let them make their impression without the compulsion of his persuasive, or worried, or angry presence. The *sending* of a letter implies the hope of a reply, by letter or word of mouth. And that is the purpose of Paul's letters. They are not, by intention, prophetic utterances, holy and valid for all time, to be received with awe and unquestioning respect by the faithful. They are the interchange of responses between members of a community. In almost every Pauline letter, the author associates others with him in writing, and in many of them he is joined by others in the final greetings. In Romans, which is deliberately a personal approach to a previously unvisited Church, Paul's name is not joined with others. And that is compensated at the end by the wealth of greetings to many friends in the Church.

At the beginning of Ephesians no one is associated with Paul, though Tychicus (from Colossians) turns up at Ephesians 6:21. Nor are there co-writers of the Pastoral Epistles. Other New Testament letters have also moved over to the solitary, authoritarian writer (1 and 2 Peter and Jude; James; 2 and 3 John; but 1 John, though obviously written by a single author (2:1), begins 'We are writing this that your joy may be complete).

1 THESSALONIANS

Paul and two colleagues write to the Christian community in Thessalonica in Macedonia (northern Greece), a large city on the Via Egnatia, the great Roman road running from the Adriatic to the Black Sea. Acts 16 – 20 tells the story of Paul's extraordinary evangelising in the Aegean area, with 17:1–10 telling of his first contact with Thessalonica. If Paul became a Christian in 31 CE, then in twenty years the Jesus story had been taken round the eastern Mediterranean – a story that concerned crucifixion (detestable to all hearers) and resurrection (ridiculous to Greeks at least, Acts 17:32) – with Christian communities as the result. 'Community', less formal than 'Church', represents *ecclesia*, a common Greek word for a public assembly, hence the need to say 'church of the Thessalonians who belong to God our Father and the Lord Jesus Christ'.

That at once throws us into theology – which can be explained fairly simply. According to venerable ideas in the ancient world, *deity* had two functions: creative and directing. Christian teachers held that God reserved the creative function wholly to himself and, in that respect (following the example of Jesus), was called Father. But he devolved the directing function to Jesus by appointing him Lord. ('Christos' means appointed; 'Lord' means one who protects, directs and corrects.) Reflect on the interplay between Father and Lord in 3:11–13.

In every letter Paul wishes his readers grace and peace. These are foundation words in Paul's theology: *grace* indicates the enormous divine generosity; *peace* asserts the comprehensive well-being in the gift of God. Experienced on the human side, *grace* is what enables you to do what otherwise you could not, and *peace* is the sense that all will be well for here is someone in control.

Most of Paul's letters continue by *thanking* God (or blessing him, the Hebrew equivalent) – very prominently in this letter (2:13; 3:9; 5:18). Put that alongside the positive responses of the Thessalonian community in 1:3–10 – despite their suffering in 1:6, 2:14 and 3:4; matched by Paul's suffering in 2:2, 9, 18; 3:1, 5, 7. To that must be added Paul's distress at his own Jewish people who killed the Lord Jesus and the prophets, drove Paul out, displeased God, are opposed to everyone, hinder Paul from offering salvation to the Gentiles, constantly filling up the measure of their own sins – but now God's anger has overtaken them at last (2:15–16).

That needs explanation because God is a *loving* God who exercises his love in a hostile world, who has *chosen* his people and selected them to be loved (1:4). That Gospel (encouraging report) is not merely a verbal statement of God's good will but is accompanied by necessary power, the Holy Spirit, and strong conviction (1:5). But simply to suppose a loving God in a hostile world will not do. He is a true and living God and sooner or later must display his anger – not at insults to his majesty, not even at the death of his Son, but at what is being done to or withheld from the people he loves. God appointed Jesus as his Son, that is, his fully empowered representative as directing Lord. He died, but God raised him from the dead; sooner or later he will return with all who are his (3:13) and will rescue us from the consequences of the anger in our hostile world (1:9–10). In the meantime the Lord is active through the Holy Spirit, one of whose activities is to promote *prophets* (of whom Paul is one) by whom the word of human beings becomes the word of God (2:13) – not mere words but in the power of the Holy Spirit (1:5). You should notice how strongly Paul insists that his special status is no barrier between him and Thessalonian Christians. He deals with them as a father deals with his children, in a way modelled on God (2:6–8).

So, believers had to wait expectantly for God's Son from heaven

(1:10). That is the Gospel of God (2:2, 8, 9) with which Paul, despite opposition, was entrusted (2:2, 4).

In call this, awareness of God is dominant. Christian communities are Churches of God (2:14). Paul's colleagues are fellow workers with God (3:2). God directs the way (3:11), tests our hearts (2:4), is Paul's witness (2:5, 10). We live to please God (4:1), live worthily of him (2:12), and rejoice before him (3:9). These very general statements are made practical by the rules that Paul gave them 'in the name of the Lord Jesus' (4:2) acting as a prophet moved by the Holy Spirit (4:8). God's will is holiness, not impurity; self-mastery; the rights of fellow Christians, and mutual love (4:3–9). The Christian ambition is to live quietly, attend to your own affairs, work with your hands, command the respect of non-Christians, and require no outside help.

For a moment it is worth pausing to notice that translation itself may be adding to the text or changing its meaning. In the NRSV, keep an eye on 4:4: 'that each one of you know how to control your own body in holiness and honour'. Is Paul talking about bodily control, or demanding that men should hallow and honour their wives, not treat them as objects of lust? Is he using a common Greek word, that elsewhere means 'vessel', as a metaphor for the human body or for a man's wife?

Paul says that these northern Greeks had turned from idols to serve a true and living God (1:9). Idols had to be bribed or placated (or so it seemed to Jews) so that people could survive, even prosper, in this world as it is. But a true and living God changes the world. Paul expected a decisive change to take place soon (and he probably said so) with the return of the risen Son of God and the operation of God's anger. But Paul's readers were worried about those who had died before the transformation. In 4:13–18 Paul offers an imaginative answer which is to be probed for its significance but is not to be regarded literally. (Paul was somewhat given to visions and revelations of the Lord, 2 Cor. 12:1.) God, with his archangels and the necessary trumpet calls, moves against the corrupted world. But first they rescue the victims: the Christian dead and the living survivors who all are – and always have been – under the protection, direction and correction of the Lord. This happens in mid-air – comical to a literal imagination – because live and dead Christians are not picked out of the mire, but all enabled to move towards the Lord as he moves towards them.

Exactly when all this would happen was unknown. The day of the Lord (an Old Testament expression, made grim by the prophet's insistence that it was darkness, not light: Amos 5:18) would be sudden and unexpected. But Christians belong to the light. God's anger is not directed against them but for them. All they need to keep them going is faith, love and hope. The death and resurrection of Christ ensures that whether Christians are awake or asleep (alive or dead) they will live with him.

Paul ends his letter in chapter 5 by courteously addressing good advice to a competent Christian community that had produced its own leaders. The instructions are not extracted from the teaching of Jesus but are tightly bound up with him: 'in the Lord' (v. 12); 'the will of God in Christ Jesus' (v. 18); 'do not quench the Spirit' (v. 19); 'the God of peace . . . at the coming of our Lord Jesus Christ' (v. 23); 'by the Lord' (v. 27); and 'the Lord Jesus Christ' (v. 28). Paul cannot give effective advice unless he holds together God, Christ and Spirit.

2 THESSALONIANS

This is so similar to the first letter in much of its wording, but so puzzling in the first part of chapter 2, that some experts regard it as a late forgery. If so, the forger was incompetent. It is better to take this letter as Paul's response to anxieties that had suddenly increased. Read the letter through and you will see how greatly the community was suffering, how much it needed encouragement – including the punishment of their tormentors (1:3–7, 11–12; 2:13–17; 3:1–5). In the first letter, Paul had urged them to wait expectantly for God's Son from heaven, and had warned them that the day of the Lord would come suddenly like a thief in the night – though it would not surprise Christians (1 Thess. 5:2, 5). Ever since, in the eighth century BCE, Amos had said that the day of the Lord would be darkness and not light, the prophetic writers had repeated the warning. Perhaps then the dreadful things now happening meant that the day had come? To which Paul responds: 'Do not be alarmed by any prophetic utterance, any pronouncement, or any letter purporting to come from us, alleging that the day of the Lord is already here' (2:2). However hurtful their present sufferings may be, something much more drastic is in preparation for the Mediterranean world. When Paul is excited by the Holy Spirit he goes for grandeur: 'the Lord Jesus revealed from heaven with his mighty angels in blazing fire'; 'the splendour of God's might . . . his glory . . . and his majesty'; 'that you might come to possess the splendour of our Lord Jesus Christ'. That high-flown language is to be read seriously but not literally; and much the same is true of the threats against wicked people in 1:8–9 and 2:3, 8, 10. For Paul, believing in God and recognising the destructiveness of extreme wickedness are of maximum importance.

Paul applies visionary language to the situation and does not avoid the confusion that visions often have. But it can be sorted out – like this (referring to verses in chapter 2):

> Already the secret forces of wickedness are at work (v. 7). There are people who have not believed the truth but have made sinfulness their choice (v. 12). They are doomed to destruction because they did not open their minds to love of the truth and so find salvation (v. 10). Since they have made that kind of choice 'God puts them under a compelling delusion, which makes them believe what is false' (v. 11). That, by the way, is the meaning that Paul gives to the anger of God: he makes them take the consequences of their deliberate choice.
>
> And so things will get worse, but at present there is a 'restraining power' (he means God) which ensures that the Horror 'will be revealed only at his appointed time' (v. 6). But when 'the restraining hand is removed' (v. 7), then 'the final rebellion against God' will take place, 'wickedness will be revealed in human form, the man doomed to destruction' (v. 3), the adversary of all deity and devotion, even enthroning himself on God's temple claiming to be God (v. 4). That is a Jewish folk memory – of the Syrian Emperor who, two hundred years earlier, had desecrated the Jerusalem Temple – revived only nine years earlier by the Roman Emperor Caligula who nearly succeeded in setting up an image of himself in the Temple. 'The coming of the wicked one is the work of Satan', accompanied by attractive but delusive promises (v. 9), but the Lord Jesus will destroy the wicked one 'with the breath of his mouth and annihilate by the radiance of his presence' (v. 8).

Something like what Paul expected took place when Jerusalem was destroyed twenty years later. For us these horrors are all too familiar.

Paul ends the letter with some sensible advice to a disturbed and worried community.

1 CORINTHIANS

Paul's preaching founded the Church at Corinth in southern Greece (Acts 18:1–18). His later relations with the Christians there and with other missionaries (e.g. Apollos and Cephas – the Hebrew name of Peter) were lively, provocative and sometimes extremely painful. But it prompted some of his most creative theological and moral responses. Before 1 Corinthians there had been a previous letter (as is clear from 1 Cor. 5:9); and from 2 Corinthians 2:4 and 7:8 we learn of an emotional and hurtful letter – which is certainly not 1 Corinthians. This letter was prompted by two matters. First, information Paul had received about quarrels in the community (1:11), cases of sexual immorality (5:1), Christians in dispute before pagan courts (6:1), divisions at the Lord's Supper (11:18), and denial of the resurrection (15:12). Second, written questions from the community about marriage (7:1), food consecrated to heathen deities (8:1), gifts of the Spirit (12:1), and about the collection in aid of God's people (16:1).

To have combined such a miscellany of reports and questions into a structured whole is an indication of Paul's mental and pastoral ability. As in the Thessalonian letters, Christians are waiting expectantly: 1:7; 4:5; 5:5; 7:29–31 ('the world as we know it is passing away'); 10:11–13; 11:26 ('Every time you eat this bread and drink the cup, you proclaim the death of the Lord, until he comes'); 15:23–24; 16:22. But more can now be said. Essentially the letter begins with Christ crucified (1:10 – 4:20) and ends with Christ risen (ch. 15), who is called 'the last Adam' (i.e., the final blueprint of humanity), who has become a life-giving spirit. Decoded, that implies that Christians, in their time of waiting, can live only by death and resurrection, guided always by the Spirit (mentioned constantly in chapters 2–7 and 12–14). They must do what is right, sometimes acceptably, sometimes not (hence Paul's experience in 4:9–13), but failure can be expected – though new life will spring up where the old endeavours failed. And throughout they will be prompted and revived by the Spirit. If the old question is asked, 'Why did the Son of God have to die?', it is answered in this letter: 'To show how faithful sons and daughters of God can survive in the world as it is, until the world is transformed.'

1:10 – 4:20

When the Gospel moved from Jewish groups (mainly interested in obedient behaviour) to Greek groups (more attracted by imaginative thought), lively disputes could be expected. The Corinthian Church founded by Paul, the Hellenistic Jew from Tarsus, had been visited by the Jewish apostle Cephas (the Hebrew form of Peter – see 1:12; 3:22; 9:5; and 15:5 where he is the first witness of the risen Christ) and by Apollos, according to Acts 18:24 the freelance Hellenistic Jew from Alexandria (1:12; 3:4–6, 22; 4:6; 16:12). The Corinthian Greeks in their church life naturally formed rival parties round their baptismal sponsors. Later it will be shown that they also behaved inappropriately at public worship and badly at the Lord's Supper. In their social life they vigorously pursued wisdom which (in this context) means thrusting know-how in a competitive society. With tactful firmness Paul treats them as his fractious but beloved family who are called to share in the life of God's Son (1:9).

Chapters 5–6
More severely, he reproves their sexual misbehaviour, their social immorality, their willingness to take fellow Christians to pagan courts, and insists that their bodily activities must honour God.

Chapter 7
Some Corinthian Christians wish to prohibit sexual intercourse. Paul agrees that the world as they know it is passing away and he wants them to be free from anxious care (7:31–32). So he gives sensible advice about those proposing marriage, about divorce, about the mutual relation of husbands and wives, and about making the best of their present conditions.

Chapters 8–10
Then he turns to responses that Christian converts should make to the continuing demands of dominant pagan religion, for example when they buy in the meat markets or are invited to a meal with unbelievers (since the meat will nominally have been offered in sacrifice). Are not Christians free from paganism? And what are the limits and outreach of that freedom?

Chapter 11
More important is the proper conduct of Christian worship in the house church(es). Unlike synagogue practice, both men and women pray and prophesy. 'In the Lord's fellowship woman is as essential to man as man to woman' (11:11). But in the Near Eastern tradition, the husband is the *public* head (promoter and defender) of the family; the wife is the *private* head of the family. If now wives are rightly praying and prophesying in public, they should wear head coverings as a sign of respect for their private headship. That may still be a sensible instruction for the Near Eastern world (though Paul

blusters in some embarrassment): for us it makes us consider our respect for women. And indeed, respect for other groups within the Church – for the Corinthians were using the Lord's Supper for a set of private parties. Paul here gives the earliest written account of the Last Supper and its proper celebration.

Chapters 12–14

The community life of Christians is marked by a great variety of spiritual gifts. They may lead to disorder and confusion unless they contribute to the life of the Church as one Christian body, with mutual love at the centre. Community worship expresses the energy and variety of spiritual experience only if it is constructive, coherent and courteous.

Chapter 15

Here is the earliest written evidence of Christ's resurrection: 'sown a physical body, raised a spiritual body' (15:44). 'The resurrection of the dead', however, perplexes the Corinthian Church and Paul works out a set of answers in reply.

Chapter 16

This concerns the collection, from Corinth and other Churches, to help distressed Christians in Jerusalem.

2 CORINTHIANS

This is best regarded as a combination of three letters: chapters 1–8, 9 and 10–13, written in that order. Paul's position in the community is, at one and the same time, essential, disputed by rivals and derided. Hence chapters 1–8 provide some of the most perplexing, chapters 10–13 some of the most hurtful reading in the New Testament. You will not go far wrong, however, if you realise that Paul is under pressure to explore the many possibilities of death and resurrection, under the prompting of the Spirit.

1:3–11

Paul had thought he was dying (v. 8) but had come to see that the consolation (or encouragement) he then received (at least partly from the many people praying for his deliverance) made him able to console (or encourage) others. Consolation or encouragement (the

Greek word can express both meanings) again becomes prominent in chapter 7.

1:12 – 2:17

As we read on, it begins to appear that Paul is defending himself against attacks that have distressed him and derided his Gospel. His dealings with Corinth (it was being said) were insincere, prompted by worldly wisdom (1:12). His letters were deliberately evasive and obscure (1:13–14) – indeed, abusive and painful (2:4; 7:8), like his last visit to Corinth (2:1). And now there was this devious change of plans (1:15 – 2:4). In any case he should have had letters of introduction (3:1 – perhaps from the Christians in Jerusalem or Antioch); but in fact he proclaims and commends himself (4:5; 5:12). He adulterates the word of God for profit (2:17). He practises cunning and distorts the word of God, while his own Gospel is suspiciously veiled (4:2–3). Such open hostility suggests that Jewish Christians who wished to remain devout followers of the Mosaic Law had come to Corinth and were pulling the Church in their direction. At least one person had gone too far, and had been penalised by the church meeting – which is now urged by Paul to forgive him (2:5–11). Why? Because as an apostle he is bound to endure suffering: like a captive prisoner in Christ's triumphant procession (2:14).

3:1 – 4:6

Paul now turns from defence to attack, and begins to write with an orator's wit and skill. He can produce (he says) impressions of the Spirit on human hearts, and needs no impressions written with ink on papyrus – not even the Mosaic Law engraved on stone. As an apostle he is empowered by God to be minister of a new covenant, not written but spiritual. (*Covenant* means a pledge of protection and support in response to a pledge of loyalty and gratitude.) The old covenant was indeed glorious (though it was a fading glory) – so glorious that Moses had to veil his face (Exod. 34:33–35). But Paul's new covenant is not veiled (as his critics say), for in the Lord Jesus we see the mirror image of the glory of God (3:18; 4:4, 6).

4:7 – 5:20

Paul has been defending not himself but the power of the Gospel. Indeed he is as fragile as an earthenware jar, continuously in danger. That must be accepted by an apostle of Jesus who died and was raised to life. 'Our troubles are slight and shortlived' (4:17). The earlier anxiety about dying (1:8) is replaced by confidence that life after death will not be the insubstantial, shadowy existence of older Jewish belief. Nor will it be the nakedness of a newborn child but (as it were) a clothed bodily structure appropriate to spiritual, immaterial life.

5:11 – 6:2
Paul now appeals for his readers to accept him as Christ's ambassador (5:20) and to understand the immense simplicity of the Gospel. Christ's death implies the death of all humankind (5:14). The sinless Christ was made one with human sinfulness, so that in his resurrection we all might be made one with the saving goodness of God (5:21). There is a new creation, the old order has gone; a new order has already begun (5:17) – in which those who live should cease to live for themselves, and should live for him who for their sakes died and was raised to life. Paul pleads for his readers to cease their hostility to God (which makes them sinners) and be reconciled to him. Incidentally, it is the new order that makes the Mosaic Law ineffective and requires the gifts of the Holy Spirit (6:6).

6:3 – 7:16
Then Paul opens his heart to the friends in Corinth with a moving account of the ambiguity of apostolic ministry (6:4–13). He urges them to keep apart from pagan idolatry (6:14 – 7:1), makes a handsome apology for the distress he had caused them, and declares his complete confidence in them (7:2–16).

8:1–24
At this time Paul was persuading the Aegean Churches to raise a substantial fund to help needy Christians in Jerusalem – and also to make links between Gentile Christians and the Jewish mother Church. This lesson in the art of persuasion includes (v. 9) one of his most illuminating statements about the relation between Christ and Christians.

9:1–14
This looks like a tactful encouragement when the Corinthian contribution seemed to be deficient.

Chapters 10–13
With chapter 10 there is a violent change of mood, from persuasion to denunciation. It is entirely unexpected and difficult to explain. It

may perhaps be Paul's response to surprising, unpleasant news from Corinth; or it may be an earlier or later letter that has lost its beginning.

The whole passage should be read aloud, giving full effect to the sarcasm, indignation and bitterness that Paul directed to the 'super-apostles' (11:5). These were religious enthusiasts (not Peter and his companions) who had entered the Corinthian community and were denigrating not only Paul but (more seriously) his understanding of the apostolic ministry. In their view, the real Jewish apostle is self-promoting, marked by courage, personal authority and self-assurance, given to visions and revelations, and expecting payment. But that, says Paul, proclaims another Jesus, a different Spirit and a different Gospel (11:4), not the Christ who 'died on the cross in weakness, but lives by the power of God' (13:4).

Paul, they say, is timid when present but courageous when else-where (10:1). His letters are weighty and powerful; but when he is present he is unimpressive, and as a speaker he is beneath contempt (10:10). In 11:22 – 12:13 Paul discloses his apostolic record from its Hebrew beginnings, through a Christian life of astonishing endurance, pastoral concern, visions and revelations to a chronic condition that persuaded him that 'when I am weak, then I am strong' (12:10).

Finally, in 12:14 – 13:14, he explores the prospect of a third visit to the Church of Corinth.

GALATIANS

The Churches of Galatia were somewhere in the middle of Asia Minor (perhaps in the region of Ankara in modern Turkey). Paul had brought them the Gospel (4:13–14) so that the blessing of Abraham should in Jesus Christ be extended to the Gentiles when they received the promised Spirit by faith (3:14). There must have been a good Jewish component in these Churches for they had learnt to say 'Abba, Father!' (4:6) and Paul expected them to understand arguments based on Abraham and the giving of the Mosaic Law. But there were some who were now trying to force circumcision upon them (6:12). That is, Gentile converts were to become Jewish Christians, and if they accepted circumcision they would be under obligation to keep the entire Law (5:3). But keeping the entire Law separates (and is intended to separate) believers from other people; whereas relying on the death and resurrection of Jesus (1:1; 2:20; 3:1; 6:14) and the gift of the Spirit (evident in chs 4–6) allows believers to experience human freedom.

1:1 – 2:14

Paul begins by rebuking his readers for abandoning the true Gospel for a non-gospel, and by outlining his relations with the Jerusalem apostles – from initial hostility, through conversion and agreement, to the decisive quarrel with Peter at Antioch – all of which has a bearing on the Galatians' present dispute.

2:15–21

Paul's response is emotional and complex. Often we have to guess what were the hostile remarks to which he is replying. But the essence of the reply is this:

> You are not behaving acceptably in God's world if you keep the Mosaic Law, however rigorously. (Paul had discovered that for himself, let alone read it in scripture, e.g. Psalm 143.)
>
> You can remain a Jew and keep the Law, or remain a Gentile under no pressure from the Law – so long as you put reliance in Christ Jesus, accepting in your life something that corresponds to his death and resurrection.

3:1 – 4:31

Eight paragraphs of argument, example and explanation.

3:1–5

They had received the gift of the Spirit by believing the Gospel, not by obeying the Law.

3:6–14

Abraham, the great forefather of Israel, was acceptable to God by faith.

3:15–18

The example of human inheritance.

3:19–25

Why the Law was given.

3:26–29

Baptism makes us all one in Christ Jesus.

4:1–11

From slavery to sonship.

4:12–20
A personal appeal.

4.21–31
As an afterthought, a return to Abraham with an imaginative interpretation of part of that story, ending with 'It is for freedom that Christ set us free' (5:1).

The rest of the letter is concerned with that freedom, what will damage it and what will promote it. This letter does not repeat what was said in previous letters about the expected day of the Lord, of the world as we know it passing away; but there is something equally striking: 'the world is crucified to me and I to the world' (6:14).

ROMANS

Paul's apostolic ministry was developed in the eastern Mediterranean, but some time in the middle 50s he decided to transfer to Spain at the western end. He wrote to the already existing Church in Rome, where he had numerous colleagues and friends, for three reasons: first, to bring his experience to bear on some contentious problems within the Roman community (chs 12–16); second, to share with them his anxiety about the Jewish people and the Christian community in Jerusalem (mainly chs 9–11); and third, to enlist Roman support for his venture to the West – if, that is, they were at one with him in understanding the Gospel (chs 1–8).

1:16–17
Paul announces his main theme in a markedly personal manner. By 'the Gospel', as we should now know, he means the death and resurrection of Jesus Christ and the gift of the Spirit. For anyone who relies on that it becomes 'the saving power of God'. Salvation is the possibility of living without reproach in a community where you wholeheartedly love God and love your neighbour as yourself. The 'righteousness of God' (i.e., his saving goodness) is available to a life that begins and ends in faith – to 'the Jew first, but the Greek also'. This letter is about the predicament of the human race, skewed in a particular way because Jesus was a Jew and because the world (as Paul's generation knew it) was coming to an end.

1:18 – 3:20
Paul vigorously denounces the wrongdoings of Gentiles and Jews, but insists that possession of the Law 'brings only consciousness of sin', that is, awareness of being on the wrong course and unable to get on the right course.

3:21 – 4:25
For that predicament of human society Paul offers the saving goodness of God in Christ Jesus, available for Jews and Gentiles. It is an 'act of liberation', a means by which atonement can be made (i.e., what is wrong can be put right) if accepted by faith (3:21–26). Faith is shown to be the essential response by the story of Abraham, the founding father of Israel and related nations.

5:1 – 8:1
Paul tells his readers that they are at peace with God, reconciled to him, their former enmity removed (5:1, 10). This has been done by death, resurrection and the Holy Spirit – symbolically represented in baptism (6:1–11) – all the work of a loving God, proved by Christ's dying for us when we were yet sinners (5:5–8). God acts towards us with graciousness, freely gives us eternal life, and rescues us from death (5:15, 21; 6:23; 7:25). Why then do we have present sufferings (5:3)?

Because the human situation is warped. There is a warp in social conditions that makes even the best intentions go wrong. Or it is like a parasite existing on God's power, using it and finally perverting it. Or, to use personal imagery, it is like a slave-master using God's law to strengthen his power, and finally working his slaves to death. Paul calls this perversion by the technical word 'sin'. He has plenty of other words for particular wrongdoings, but he uses 'sin' to indicate that human existence invariably goes off target. It is the result of Adam's disastrous but inevitable choice in the allegorical story of the garden of Eden. Eating the fruit of the symbolic tree would give knowledge of good and evil, that is, what enhances life and what destroys it. So the choice was this: human beings would make no decisions but would be wholly cared for by God, or they would make their own decisions and take the consequences. So they became slaves to sin (6:17). The law of God is unquestionably spiritual and admirable: the earnest believer may long to obey it. But (says Paul), 'When I want to do right, only wrong is within my reach' (7:21). The only way to be rid of sin's power is to die – and begin anew 'alive to God in Christ Jesus' – as is signified in baptism (6:3–4).

8:2–39
At last Paul comes to Spirit (the power of God to bring new life out of disaster), in contrast to the weak and fallible 'flesh' (our self-regarding and self-destructive manner of living in community). And then, with that ever-dominant sense that the present world is passing away, he contrasts present sufferings with the glory to be revealed.

Chapters 9–11
If all this is true, it leaves Paul with a major problem: why have the Jewish people, by and large, not accepted the Gospel? What about God's special care for Israel, going back to his promises to Abraham? So Paul begins, with no little anxiety, to explore God's irreproachable freedom (granted that he has made promises) to shape the course of human history in a sin-enslaved world. In such affairs God is like a master craftsman, making instruments for creative or destructive use (referring to social communities, not individual people). The way of faith is clear and available (10:6–10) but the response of believing Israel is at best uncertain – to be left, in the end, to the mysterious greatness of God (11:33–36).

Chapters 12–16
The Roman Church: its communal life, relation to the state, internal disputes, and membership.

PHILIPPIANS

This letter, written from prison (possibly but not certainly in Rome), was intended to thank the Philippian Church for their support and to encourage them in their own need. The recognisably Pauline themes are writ large, particularly death and resurrection. The model is Christ Jesus: being in the form of God, he made himself a slave, even to the point of death – and then was raised to the heights (2:6–11).

Paul imprisoned can now scarcely act as an apostle, but fellow Christians become confident to speak the word of God fearlessly. Paul is willing to die, but perhaps he should struggle on. To Jewish opponents he asserts his thorough Jewish qualities – but writes them off because of Christ (that is a kind of dying), in order to know Christ and the power of his resurrection (3:4–11). At present he is supported by the Spirit (1:19; 2:1; 3:3), 'forgetting what is behind and straining towards what lies ahead' (3:13), for 'we expect our deliverer to come' (3:20), and 'the Lord is near' (4:5).

PHILEMON

Paul in prison has come across and converted a runaway slave called Onesimus who belongs to Philemon (also a Pauline convert) who is a member of the Christian community of Colossae (on the evidence of Philemon 2 and 10 compared with Colossians 4:9 and 17). For Paul the major change taking place in his world was the inclusion of Jew and Gentile in one community of faith. He could not prejudice that change by denouncing slavery, but he could send Onesimus back as more than a slave, as a brother dear to Paul and to his owner.

COLOSSIANS

When this letter was sent to Colossae (and another, now lost, to Laodicea, 4:16) Paul was in prison (4:10, 18). The two towns, about a hundred miles due east of Ephesus on the west coast of Asia Minor (modern Turkey), had been evangelised by Epaphras (1:7; 4:12), not by Paul – they had not set eyes on him (2:1). But it may have seemed to them that Paul's evangelism was falling apart, so this letter assures them that 'the gospel is bearing fruit and making new growth the whole world over' (1:6), and that Paul's present suffering is a necessary and effective supplement to the past suffering of Christ (1:24). All this – in opposition to people who are making demands for ritual practices and abstentions (2:16–23).

It cannot confidently be said whether this letter was composed by Paul, or drafted with his approval, or put out in Paul's name to support the teaching of Epaphras. Some standard Pauline themes are present. The oneness in Christ of Jew and Gentile, circumcised and uncircumcised is explicit in 3:11, and underlies much of the letter. The Spirit is mentioned, but only once, in 1:8. Death and resurrection are very prominent: 1:18, 20, 22; 2:20. But the resurrection of Christians has already happened (3:1–4); they have been brought into the Kingdom of God's dear Son (1:13), and brought to fulfilment (2:10). Christian hope sets the tone of the letter (1:5, 23, 27), but not, it seems, as an expectation of historical change. The background is not history but the created universe of heaven and earth, one continuum in which the reconciliation drama takes place (1:5, 16, 20). Since the cosmic powers have been overcome and humiliated (2:15), the business of Christians is to develop the appropriate wisdom, matched by generous and loving conduct (3:5 – 4:5). Responsibilities in a Christian household are set out (3:18 – 4:1) in a Christian adaptation of the standard rules of Greek family life, intended to preserve the established order of society. Much the same appears (more elaborately) in Ephesians 5:21 – 6:9 where more information will be found.

5 The Historical Dividing Line

SAYINGS AND GOSPELS

At this point we must take account of public events. In 66 CE the Jewish people rebelled against the Roman government. In 70, after a long siege, Jerusalem fell. Its people were killed or removed, and the city was destroyed. By that time (according to ancient tradition) Peter and Paul were dead. All the remaining New Testament writings must have been composed with those deaths and that destruction in mind.

Look first at the gospels, all written in Greek with only occasional examples of Aramaic, the common language of Palestine – though the country was effectively bilingual. Matthew, Mark and Luke are written in similar style, quite different from John. Mark, the shortest, is mostly reproduced in Matthew, and largely reproduced in Luke. Detailed examination of the Greek texts proves that the similarities arose not from memory but from copying. Of the various possibilities, the best solution is that Matthew and Luke independently used Mark (with more or less freedom) as the basis of their gospels. Thus Mark was the inventor of the 'gospel', which was something other than simple story-telling.

MARK

Nothing in Matthew, Mark or Luke identifies the authors, so we depend upon tradition. In an early third-century church history it is reported that Papias, Bishop of Hierapolis, in an early second-century book (since lost) reported the tradition that Mark, having been the interpreter of Peter, wrote down accurately, but not in order, all that he remembered of the Lord's sayings and doings. Mark himself had not heard the Lord nor been a follower. That not very intelligent tradition (devised by people devoted to the more elaborate gospels of Matthew and Luke) at least produces the name Mark – which appears several times in the New Testament, sometimes as John Mark. If the name always refers to the same person, then we have this information: he was a member of the early Christian community in Jerusalem; through his cousin Barnabas, he became an assistant when Barnabas and Paul were evangelising Cyprus, but later left them – to Paul's disapproval (Acts 12:12, 25; 13:5, 13; 15:37–39). Later still, he turns up as a companion of Paul (Philemon 24; Col. 4:10; 2 Tim. 4:11), and even of Peter (1 Pet. 5:13).

Paul's letters constantly refer to the death and resurrection of Jesus, but very seldom mention anything else he did or said. But there must have been a large stock of memories, even of the simple kind ascribed to Peter in Acts 10:34–43. What Mark did was to select and arrange such memories and make from them an artfully planned story, from apparent success to seeming failure. *When* he did so is not known, but the extraordinary warnings in chapter 13 either look forward to the revolt against Rome or backward on the ruin of Jerusalem. Hence the date of Mark's gospel would be between 65 and 75.

Why Mark devised a 'gospel' is probably hinted at in its original ending: 'They said nothing to anyone, for they were afraid' (16:8). All translations of the gospel continue with verses 9–20, normally with a warning that (on the evidence of ancient manuscripts, translations and references) they were not written by Mark. Did he, perhaps, write his own ending which was lost, or was he prevented from completing his script? Or did he intend that abrupt, provocative ending? If the women believed that the 'criminal' executed by the Romans was in fact alive, it would be highly dangerous to say so. Of course they said nothing, because they were afraid. Now, however, was the time not only to speak but also for Mark to write. Not only were Peter and Paul dead, their apostolic missions to Jews and Gentiles now precarious, but others were pushing their versions of the truth. To put the Gospel in writing would give it a power of its own, thus defining and promoting 'the Way' as the Christian movement was being called.

In the first instance Mark wrote for people who were familiar with the topography of Palestine. He mentions regions and place names. Sometimes the readers need to know the countryside if they are properly to grasp what is written. Of chief importance is Galilee – hill country with villages, including Nazareth – especially the Sea of Galilee, with various lakeside events and boat journeys, with the mention of Bethsaida, Gennesareth, Dalmanutha (long-ago forgotten), and Capernaum with its custom house. Well to the north is Caesarea Philippi, and well to the north-west on the sea coast are Tyre and Sidon. Flowing south from the Sea of Galilee is the Jordan river, and somewhat to the south and east of Galilee is the Decapolis (a league of mainly Greek towns, including Gadara or perhaps Gerasa). Further south is Transjordan, where uninhabited parts of the country-side are sometimes called 'the wilderness', though much of the valley was green and fertile. South of Galilee, on the west bank was Samaria (which Mark does not mention) and Judaea with Jericho, Jerusalem and the Temple, Bethphage (pronounced 'Beth-faggy') and Bethany, the Mount of Olives and Golgotha. Far south was Idumaea, from which the Herods came.

In reading the gospel you can follow Jesus as he moves from the Jordan wilderness to Galilee, sometimes in the hill-country villages, more often by the lakeside – either on the well-inhabited west bank or the remoter east bank. And you will notice his ventures outside Galilee to non-Jewish territory: to the Decapolis (ch. 5), to the territory of Tyre and Sidon (ch. 7), even to Caesarea Philippi (ch. 8) – before turning back and going up to Jerusalem (in Mark, for the only time).

Why was such topographical information provided, in a book that was launched when Peter and Paul were dead, Jerusalem was in ruins, and the Christian movement was established around the eastern Mediterranean? Surely to preserve the link between the Churches and the reality of Jesus who was a Galilean, not a Jerusalemite; who demonstrated God's kingship over physical and spiritual infestation; who indeed devoted himself to his fellow Jews but indicated, by his excursions outside Jewish territory, that Gentiles also could be offered the Gospel. The Galilean expanse of water was normally called the *Lake* of Gennesaret or of Tiberias: Mark always calls it the *Sea* of Galilee. Why? Because symbolically it represents the voyages and storms of the Mediterranean and points to the ministry of Jesus (who comes to them walking on the water) in the Pauline, and no doubt Petrine, Churches.

1:1–13

Here John baptises in the wilderness (this explains why the Christian Way begins with baptism, as in 1 Corinthians and Romans). In 10: 38–39 Jesus' baptism points to his death. The Spirit descends on Jesus and identifies him as Son of God. In Paul, sons of God are endowed with Spirit. 'Son of God' (the commonest designation of Jesus in Paul) appears seldom in Mark (by unclean spirits, 3:11; 5:7; by the voice at the Transfiguration 9:7, and by a foreign soldier, 15:39). The Spirit (dominant in Paul) is also seldom in Mark: apart from David's inspiration (12:36), only 3:29 (slandering the Holy Spirit) and 13:11 (for Christians speaking under interrogation). All other references are to 'unclean spirits'.

1:14 – 6:29

Crowds had flocked to John, but his arrest prompted Jesus to seek the crowds in Galilee, announcing the nearness of the Kingdom of God. Throughout this section, however, Jesus is under the shadow of John – though whereas John's disciples fasted, the disciples of Jesus did not (2:18–20). But John's death at the hands of Herod (6:14–29) was an ominous sign to Jesus who was later compared to John (8:28). Later still, in conflict with the religious authorities, Jesus made their response to John the Baptist the touchstone of their sincerity (11:30–32).

These chapters give a vigorous impression of Jesus' varied activity: instructing and training, healing and exorcising – even restoring life to a woman and a girl! Even restoring sanity to a Gentile (5:1–43)! Even giving help on the sabbath (3:1–6)! But failing to impress his home town (6:1–6). At first sight the oddest episode is 1:21–27: Jesus frees a possessed man from an unclean spirit but the synagogue company are amazed at his *teaching*. To us that seems surprising if teaching means 'conveying information' and we forget about 'learning skills'. To put it more generally, teaching means showing people how to respond – as it does when Jesus teaches in parables, which are not illustrative stories of abstract truths but stimuli to awaken responses.

In this section there are three parables of sowing and growing. What they imply is indicated by Paul: 'The seed you sow does not come to life unless it has first died' (1 Cor. 15:36); and by John: 'Unless a grain of wheat falls into the ground and dies, it remains that and nothing more; but if it dies, it bears a rich harvest' (John 12:24). But not always: some seed may be lost, some may sprout and wither, some sprout and be choked – even though a very plentiful crop is promised. The followers of Jesus ought to know that God's Kingdom is like that – the 'interpretation' in 4:14–20 indicates that Jesus is talking about the response to God's word (i.e., instruction) by people to whom every parable is a puzzle. Not surprisingly since these parables hint at death and resurrection as the common structure of life.

In his healing and exorcising, Jesus is releasing, restoring and cleansing people so that they can respond. In 2:1–12 there is one of Mark's very few references to the forgiveness of sins – with the simple indication that sins are wicked not because they displease God but because they paralyse people.

6:30 – 8:21

This part of the gospel begins and ends with the *feeding* of great companies of people on the east side of the lake. Chapter 7 deals with the invalidity of Jewish eating rules, with a Gentile woman who wins relief for her daughter by a bold demand that her child be fed, and with the observation that 'he even makes the deaf hear and the dumb speak'. And from 8:14–21 it becomes plain that 'eating' has become a symbol for 'teaching'. The Gospel is sustenance.

8:22 – 10:52

This section turns to *seeing* or perception. It begins with the restoration of sight to a blind man at Bethsaida, just before Jesus probes the understanding of his disciples; and ends with similar restoration to a blind beggar at Jericho, just before Jesus begins the ascent to Jerusalem. These are the last two healings recorded in the gospel: only here is blindness mentioned, and nowhere else are there *two* examples of a particular cure. In this section Jesus makes three attempts to get the disciples to see what he must now do and endure, rather than move towards triumphant messiahship: 8:27–33 (Peter gets it wrong as so often in Mark); 9:30–32 (the disciples fail to understand); 10:32–40 (James and John want the privilege of protecting Jesus). Jesus insistently refers to himself as Son of Man (a human being in misery or majesty) who will serve humankind by setting them free (10:45). The forthcoming suffering is the precondition (for himself and his disciples) of the expected – and foreshadowed – triumph (9:1–8). Only in this context does Mark record the teaching of Jesus about discipleship (9:14 – 10:31).

11:1 – 14:25

In Jerusalem Jesus stages a demonstration of the coming kingdom of our father David (11:1–10) and performs a prophetic rejection of the financially powerful Temple. In utter contrast to the sowing and growing parables of chapter 4, he puts a curse on a fruitless fig tree (a symbol of Israel) and implies that the curse is effective because of his faith in God (11:12–14, 20–25). Then by dispute and parable he repudiates the chief priests, scribes and elders (the wealthy and powerful Sanhedrin, hand in glove with the Romans) in 11:27 – 12:12; and settles accounts with Pharisees and supporters of Herod; with Sadducees; and with scribes (12:13–40 – though one scribe is praised for his nearness to the Kingdom of God). In 12:41–44 the comment on the widow's penny expresses a Galilean's shock at the enormous wealth on display in Jerusalem, and it leads on to the expensive fine buildings of the Temple.

Chapter 13 is unlike anything else in the gospel. It deals with a series of events so drastic and revolutionary that nothing, in the scope of the readers' experience, will ever be the same again. It puts them on their guard against spurious leaders, warns them of violence and disaster, encourages them to stand firm, and tells them when to take refuge. What is at stake is the very existence of the world (13:24–25) and the destructive centre is the desecration and ruin of the Temple.

The reconstructive response is the coming of the Son of Man (not the Messiah of Israel) in the clouds with great power and glory (symbolic biblical language) whose authority is not local but universal (13:26–27). The fig tree (barren in chapter 11) may produce tender shoots (13:28), but no one knows when – not Jesus himself; only the Father.

14:1–25

When Passover is near, a woman extravagantly anoints Jesus, who does not repudiate her action. This anointing anticipates his burial and will be her worldwide memorial. Whereupon 'Judas Iscariot, one of the Twelve, went to the chief priests to betray him', presumably warning them not only that Jesus was hostile to their dominance of the Temple (which they already knew) but also that he expected his own death to replace the Temple sacrifices. That conjecture was confirmed when, at the Passover with the Twelve, Jesus gave an unusual significance not to the central feature (the Passover lamb which had been brought from the Temple) but to the bread as his body and the wine as his blood – not simply for the Twelve but for many.

14:26–52

In Gethsemane Jesus (accompanied by his closest disciples) three times puts to the test his conviction that he must accept the fatal cup of suffering. He discovers also that he must do so with no support from his disciples. He is then identified by Judas and, without resistance, is arrested by the Temple authorities. The young man who fled naked is an appropriate symbol of the disciples.

14:53–65
Jesus is questioned by an informal gathering of the ruling clique in Jerusalem. The informality is indicated by Peter's presence in the courtyard, by the horseplay of the attendants, and by the chaotic proceedings. The translation 'Council' in 14:55 and 15:1 is too formal. They are members of the wealthy priestly families, advisers on the Mosaic Law, and devout lay supporters. Jesus' threat to the Temple might destroy the livelihood of the thousands of priests, and ruin the prosperity of Jerusalem. So this is not a trial to discover whether Jesus is guilty or not, but the search for a plausibly legal way of putting down a Galilean dissident. It is found when Jesus (for the only time) admits that he is Messiah: he can now be handed over to the Roman authorities as an aspirant to Jewish kingship.

15:1 – 16:8
They handed him over to Pilate as a claimant to the Kingdom, and Pilate passed the expected death sentence. The story is told with maximum irony. Throughout the whole distressing story Jesus speaks only three times: in 14:62, 'I am' plus words of scripture; in 15:2, only 'Thou sayest'; in 15:34, four words of Psalm 22. All the other characters speak – and give themselves away. Peter comes off very badly – but a Gentile soldier identifies Jesus as the Son of God.

Apart from additional verses added later, the gospel originally ended with the ironical statement: 'They said nothing to anyone, for they were afraid.' There is no resurrection appearance: only an instruction to go to Galilee where he will be seen. Nothing more need be said: what Mark had written in 1:14 – 10:52 was the testimony of the living Jesus, from 'Repent, and believe the gospel' to 'Your faith has healed you'. What better support than that could be offered to the Pauline mission.

A COLLECTION OF SAYINGS

Mark's gospel set the *pattern* for the other three, even though they differ in content, arrangement and style. In Mark what Jesus said and did are presented in a narrative. Sayings and events are related to what happened before and what came after. Place, time and circumstance are part of the remembrance of Jesus. So this gospel is not a collection of sayings or episodes like the Jewish 'Sayings of the Fathers' or the early Christian Gospel of Thomas. But a very early collection of sayings of Jesus must have existed. He would normally speak in Aramaic (the common language of the country) where people trusted the remembered rather than the written word. There is no evidence of a collection of his Aramaic teaching. But Palestine was bilingual: when his teaching was turned into everyday Greek (the common language of the Roman Empire), a small written collection was possible and useful. If the gospels of Matthew and Luke are printed side by side it becomes clear not only that they report much more of Jesus' teaching than Mark does, but that independently they often produce the same sayings, sometimes in almost identical Greek. Most possibly they both used a booklet of about two hundred verses (five pages of the REB) containing *sayings* of Jesus.

MATTHEW AND LUKE

Both Matthew and Luke used Mark's gospel (though in different ways) as the narrative basis of their own gospels. Apart from the birth and resurrection stories, they add few episodes to Mark's account. Luke adds a small number; Matthew adds very few. But they both provide many additional *sayings* of Jesus – some present only in Matthew, some present only in Luke. No doubt these were sayings remembered in their respective communities. But a large collection (at least 200 verses) of the sayings of Jesus (not found in Mark) are present in both Matthew and Luke. Sometimes they are word-for-word the same, sometimes divergent forms of a common original. As an example, compare the Lord's Prayer in Matthew 6:9–13 with the much simpler form in Luke 11:2–4. Various Christian communities had their own stock of memorised sayings of Jesus. That is what Matthew and Luke add to their adaptations of Mark. In Matthew they appear in five major sections of teaching, in Luke in a long amorphous central section.

Who wrote Matthew's gospel is uncertain. The same Papias who preserved a tradition about Mark also said that 'Matthew composed the oracles in the Hebrew language and each person interpreted them as best he could' – which is not appropriate to the gospel. But there is another possible indication in Matthew 9:9 where Jesus recruits another disciple, a tax-collector called Matthew – though Mark and Luke call him Levi. And in Matthew 10:3, giving the names of the Twelve, Matthew is called 'the tax-collector' – though not in Mark or

Luke. A hint perhaps that the apostle Matthew was the author of the gospel? If so, he was a constant companion of Jesus, hearing and remembering his teaching. But would such an eye-witness have relied on Mark (who was not an eye-witness) for the historical account of Jesus, to which he added so few episodes? We cannot know *who* the author was, though we can form a good impression of what sort of person he was.

The third gospel has a self-conscious author, who has composed a book in two volumes (the gospel and Acts), both addressed to 'your excellency Theophilus' (entirely unknown) as a kind of patron. The first four verses of the gospel – a single sentence in very pompous Greek – seem to imply that there are many stories about the new Christian movement, but this account, told from inside, is the most reliable. This is a typical book dedication, an author's self-promotion – though he does not give his name. In fact there is no evidence of the author's identity until the end of the second century when Luke the physician is so named. That refers to Colossians 4:14 where the imprisoned Paul sends greetings from 'our dear friend Luke, the doctor', mentioned again in Philemon 24 (and 2 Tim. 4:10–11). In Colossians 4:11 Paul names the only Jewish Christians who are with him. Hence Luke is a Gentile Christian. If Luke is indeed the author of the gospel and Acts, he may possibly hint at his companionship with Paul when in some passages of Acts he says '*We* did such and such' instead of '*They* did so and so'.

Matthew and Luke (unlike the other two gospels) begin with birth and infancy stories, together with genealogies (which do not entirely agree). In the ancient world family origins, allegiance and responsibility were profoundly important – as when Paul describes himself as 'of the tribe of Benjamin, a Hebrew born and bred' (Phil. 3:5). To a Jewish reader, therefore, it must have sounded rather bleak when the most he said of Jesus was 'born of a woman, born under the law' (Gal. 4:4). If Jesus had a wonderful resurrection accompanied by angels, would it not be expected that his birth was also wonderful and angelic? Both Matthew and Luke, from their different positions, also want to assert the genuine Jewishness of Jesus – *that* comes from the mother – and Luke goes further, by telling of the circumcision, naming, and presentation in the Temple. Jesus is shown as a proper Jewish child of whom much is expected – twelve years later, a youngster devoted to Temple and Law.

If Joseph had been the child's father, Jesus (as first-born) would have become responsible for the progress of Joseph's family and the protection of his property, as presumably he did until the age of thirty (Luke 3:23). But then he took responsibility for the whole family of Israel, in obedience to the Father who is in heaven – because his conception had been extraordinary. Matthew very briefly attributes the conception to the Holy Spirit (the life-giver), tells how Joseph was instructed by a dream angel to provide a normal family home for Jesus, and finds a hint of the divine purpose in Isaiah 7:14. Luke's more elaborate story provides two surprising first births: one to an elderly woman, the other to her young relative (thus tying together the later followers of John and Jesus). The story-telling, moving between the Temple in Jerusalem and rural Judaea at Bethlehem, is given worldly significance by the Roman census, and heavenly significance by the numerous angelic communications. Luke (like the Pharisees but not the Sadducees, Acts 23:8) was rather fond of angels – frequent in Acts though not much in the gospel.

Matthew's story-telling is a different way of expressing the significance of the birth of Jesus, and there is no point in trying to make an historical account out of Matthew and Luke. Matthew says, in effect, that even from his birth Jesus was under threat from Jewish politicians, that God had to protect him by residence in Egypt (like Israel of old), that Judaea was never safe for him, and that Gentile wisdom (the magi) paid tribute to Jesus more readily than anything Jewish – so preparing for Matthew 28:19–20, 'Go therefore to all nations and make them my disciples.'

Something ought to be said about *the virgin birth*, which plays no part in the rest of the New Testament (though a few early Latin writers read it at John 1:13). No doubt ancient Jews and Greeks knew that children could be conceived after sexual intercourse between a man and a woman – presumably if God approved. It would not seem surprising to them if, in special cases, God approved conception without intercourse. For us today, with our modern knowledge of fertilisation and conception, that would seem not merely surprising but almost impossible – like a good many miracles. But as a matter of Christian belief we are only committed to the conviction that Jesus, born as a totally special person, entered human existence, as we all do, from a woman's womb. The birth stories are imaginative expressions of the special nature and yet real humanity of Jesus.

MATTHEW

1:1 – 2:23
Infancy stories.

3:1 – 4:11
Baptism and temptations. No one indicates why Jesus left Galilee to receive John's baptism, though Matthew says that when John demurred Jesus insisted. But we can make sense of it if we remember Luke's statement that Jesus was about thirty years old when he began his work. Since average life-expectancy in those days was twenty to twenty-five years, by the age of thirty Jesus had fulfilled responsibilities to his family and could respond to God's special call when John's baptism gave the signal. As it did.

Then the special call had to be tested – in prophetic fashion for forty days (Exod. 24:18, Moses; 1 Kings 19:8, Elijah) by Satan (as Mark says – Matthew and Luke tiresomely prefer the Greek word *diabolos*). Satan first appears in the opening chapters of the Book of Job where his function is to see if Job will break down under acute pressure. So here: will Jesus remain faithful when facing sheer hunger in Galilee, massive priestly power in Jerusalem, and insistent demands of the Gentile authorities?

4:12–25
Preaching, disciples, and healing in Galilee.

Chapters 5–7
Sermon on the Mount – with some parallels in Luke – the first of five blocks of teaching (the others are chs 10, 13, 18 and 23–25).

Like Luke's Sermon on the Plain it begins with beatitudes, that is, recipes for reliable happiness. Both writers agree that Jesus blessed the poor and needy, those who sorrow and weep, the hungry, and those who are persecuted and hated. But in Matthew the poor are 'poor in spirit' (perhaps devout but unassertive), the hungry are those who 'hunger and thirst to see right prevail', the sorrowful find consolation, and those 'persecuted in the cause of right' possess the Kingdom of Heaven. Matthew adds four more blessings: on the gentle, the merciful, the pure in heart, and the peacemakers – thus presenting Jesus as the devout Jewish moralist.

The disciples are to display such morality to the world – as salt (one of 'the basic necessities of human life', Ecclus. 39:26) and as light

('light to the nations', Isa. 49:6). Not that Jesus had come to abolish the instructions (Law) given to Moses, or their application in later times by the prophets. His purpose was to give them their full, proper effect for his own time. When he says that 'not a letter, not one stroke of a letter will pass from the law until all is accomplished' he cannot intend the rigid, literal insistence of scribes and Pharisees. For example, in Matthew 15:11 Jesus says 'No one is defiled by what goes into his mouth; only by what comes out of it' – thus, it would seem, abandoning the list of unclean foods in Leviticus 11. On the other hand, his application of the Law is more searching than the scribal interpretation. Jesus insists on the Law being fulfilled in a more imaginative way than the strict, conscientious manner of authoritative scribes and devout Pharisees. Matthew's is a Law-keeping gospel, first offered to Jews and then extended by baptism to all nations (28:19–20), perhaps a Petrine gospel in tacit opposition to Paul's refusal to fasten the Law on Gentile converts.

8:1 – 9:34
Healings, demoniac powers of storm and Gentile peoples; disciples and discipleship.

9:35 – 11:1
Sending out of disciples and instructions for their mission to the lost sheep of the house of Israel – at this stage strictly forbidding approach to Gentile or Samaritan villages.

11:2 – 12:50
Stories showing Jewish indifference or hostility to Jesus' healings and exorcisms, despite the initiative of John the Baptist, the direct prompting of the Father, Isaiah's prophecy of God's servant and the power of the Spirit.

13:1–52
Parables of the Kingdom of Heaven.

13:53 – 17:27
An edited version of Mark 6:1 – 9:32, with a very important addition in 16:17–19 making Peter the rock on which the Church is built (suggesting support for the Petrine Jewish mission rather than the Pauline), and an odd addition about the Temple tax (17:24–27).

18:1–35
A miscellaneous collection of community instructions, showing (vv. 15–20) how Matthew's community dealt with disputes.

Chapters 19–22
Mark 10 – 12 rewritten with supplementary parables.

Chapter 23
A severe attack on scribes and Pharisees, admitting the validity of their teaching but objecting to their practice and pointing to the consequences for Jerusalem: 'There is your temple, forsaken by God and laid waste' (v. 38).

24:1 – 25:13
A revision of Mark 13, plus additions (some also in Luke) and the striking parables of the Twelve Virgins and the Sheep and the Goats.

Chapters 26–27
A revision of Mark 14 – 15 with small additions.

Chapter 28
Resurrection: Mark's bleak ending is changed by an appearance of the risen Jesus, by an accusation that the chief priests had bribed the military guard to say that the body had been stolen while they slept (!), and by the departure of the Eleven to Galilee where the risen Lord commissions them to make disciples of Gentile nations (presumably countermanding the instructions of 10:5–6), to baptise them in the threefold name of God, confident that Jesus is with them until the completion of the present age (ominously foreshadowed in 24:3).

LUKE

Chapters 1–2
Infancy stories.

Chapter 3
Baptism, the Baptist, and genealogy.

4:1–13
Temptation.

4:14 – 9:50
Jesus, empowered by the Spirit, returns to Galilee. He not only teaches in synagogues with great success but also performs healings and gathers disciples. This is mainly a revision of Mark 1 – 3 with a double Lukan preface. In Luke 4:16–30 Jesus tells the people of his own hill village what he must do (reading from the scroll of Isaiah): announce good tidings for the poor, for prisoners, the blind, and broken victims. This meets with approval until Jesus deliberately mentions his work in the Gentile–Jewish town of Capernaum down by the lakeside, and reminds them that God long ago healed a non-Jewish Sidonian widow and a Syrian leper. So the good news is for both Jews and non-Jews. Then in 5:1–11 Luke inserts the story of an amazing catch of fish, when Jesus says to his disciples 'From now on you will be catching people'. Luke is thus declaring his main interest: the spread of the Gospel in Acts.

From 6:20 Luke abandons Mark for a while. He records his Sermon on the Plain where Jesus is the radical prophet rather than the moralising rabbi of the Sermon on the Mount; plus six encounter stories, some also known to Matthew. Then with 8:4, the parable of the sower, he selectively resumes Mark, omitting much of Mark 6, all of Mark 7, much of Mark 8, and some of Mark 9.

In Luke 9:51 – 18:14 the Markan narrative is again abandoned (apart from a few Markan episodes) and Luke uses the convention of a journey to bring together a great deal of Jesus' teaching and actions. In 9:51 'he set his face resolutely towards Jerusalem' and he is already in Samaria; but in 10:1 he appoints seventy-two forerunners: surely for Galilee, not Samaria, because in 13:31–33 Jesus is warned to leave Herod's territory. Luke presents this body of information in terms of a journey because he intends it to be used by the travelling evangelists of the early Church, so that 'from east and west, from north and south, people will come and take their places at the banquet in the Kingdom of God' (13:29). For the task of seeking the lost there is much instruction about the life of disciples, about healing, prayers and blessings, about signs and warnings, together with the most famous Lukan parables. A great deal of this material is also present in Matthew's gospel.

18:15 – 19:27
This section selectively rejoins Mark 10 and adds the episode of Zacchaeus and the parable of the pounds.

19:28 – 21:4
This revives Mark 11:1 – 12:44, adding a vivid prophecy of the investment and destruction of Jerusalem and (as Matthew also does) a denunciation of the Pharisees.

21:5–38
These verses revise Mark 13 and provide a special ending.

22:1 – 23:56
This is an extensive revision of Mark 14 – 15, adding the examination of Jesus by Herod, stressing the insensitive and inept behaviour of the Twelve in contrast with the grief of the daughters of Israel, rewriting the Last Supper account, and giving a nobler ending of the crucifixion.

Chapter 24
Resurrection. Luke also begins with Mark. The women, arriving early at the tomb and finding the stone rolled away, go inside and see two men in dazzling clothes who say 'Why search among the dead for one who is alive?' They should remember that, while he was still in Galilee, he had told them that the Son of Man must be crucified but would rise again on the third day. So they reported everything to the Eleven – who thought it nonsense.

Then there is the elaborate story of two disciples going to Emmaus who unknowingly encounter Jesus, are scripturally instructed by him, and finally recognise him when he breaks bread and offers it to them. Then on returning to Jerusalem they are greeted with the news that the Lord was risen and had appeared to Simon (i.e., Peter – not described – unlike the thrice-told story in Acts of the appearance to Paul). As they were then telling their own Emmaus story the Lord again appeared, showed his hands and his feet and ate a piece of cooked fish to prove that he was not a ghost. He then explained scripture to them, made them witnesses to all nations beginning from Jerusalem, but told them to wait in Jerusalem for power from above. He blessed them, and 'withdrew from them and was carried up into heaven' (as the NRSV, though not the REB, properly says). So they stayed in Jerusalem, especially frequenting the Temple.

6 The Acts of the Apostles

Paul had said that the Gospel was for the Jew first, but the Greek also (Rom. 1:16). Luke's second volume demonstrates that pattern. Chapters 1–15 are dominated by Peter: then his name disappears. As early as chapters 7 and 8 we hear of a young man named Saul who became a scourge of the Petrine community but later is converted and becomes a leading member of the Church at Antioch (on the coast, about 300 miles north of Jerusalem). That Church chooses him and Barnabas for a mission to Cyprus (where he changes the Hebraic name Saul to the Greek Paul) and to Pisidia (in modern Turkey, inland beyond the Taurus mountains). When they return to Antioch they run into a furious dispute with Jewish Christians who insist that Gentile converts must be circumcised. So Paul, Barnabas and some others set off for a conference in Jerusalem where (after powerful speeches by Peter, James the brother of Jesus, Barnabas and Paul) a compromise resolution is accepted and sent out to the Churches. Thereafter chapters 16–28 are dominated by Paul.

That pattern is obviously deliberate. Peter surely did not become a non-entity after the Jerusalem conference. At a later time it was plausible to circulate a letter written by him to Christians living in Pontus, Galatia, Cappodocia, Asia and Bithinia (1 Pet. 1:1); and his missionary travels were known to the Church of Corinth (under the name Cephas, 1 Cor. 1:12; 3:22; 9:5). According to Paul's statement in Galatians 2:7–8, it had been agreed at Jerusalem that Paul had been entrusted with taking the Gospel to the Gentiles as surely as Peter had been entrusted with taking it to the Jews. So Luke decided to write the first thirty years of the Church's history not in a neutral way but by putting a Petrine stamp on the beginning, a Pauline stamp on the ending – and a reconciling account in the middle, which demands most attention.

Why should he write an historical account at all? Among the various reasons for writing history, an important purpose is to let us know how we got where we are – and then, with that burden or that benefit, allow us to discover what we can do about our own situation. Think of Luke's situation in the early 80s. According to report, Peter and Paul had been put to death when the Emperor Nero (54–68 CE) was inflicting punishment on 'the Christians, a class of men given to new and mischievous superstition' (as a contemporary historian said). The Holy City and its Temple had been destroyed in 70: the people were impoverished and leaderless except for a group of Pharisaic teachers rebuilding Jewish life round the Law. It was reported that Jewish Christians had fled to Pella, just across Jordan in the Decapolis region. Nero's successor Vespasian, a 'wise, strong and sober Emperor' had died in 79 CE, to be succeeded by his equally able son Titus who died two years later. His brother Domitian, who was called 'Our Master and our God', raised money for his military expenses by new taxes, especially on Jews (and perhaps Christians), and he instituted a reign of terror until his death in 96 CE.

As Luke understood the apostolic commission, the Holy Spirit would bear witness to Jesus to 'the farthest corners of the earth'; and among the multilingual hearers on the day of Pentecost were 'visitors from Rome, both Jews and proselytes' (Acts 1:8; 2:5–11). In the 50s, when Gentiles became members of Christian Churches, they were strongly pressed by Jewish Christians to accept Jewish circumcision, food laws and so on. Now, after the ruin of Jerusalem, Gentile Christians were perhaps inclined to ignore the pressures and problems of Jewish Christians – as well as Jewish traditions. Therefore, what Luke attempted in Acts was to draw together Jewish and Gentile Christians by displaying the Church's origin and formative growth in Judaism, under the guidance of Peter – who was indeed the first to allow a Gentile to accept the Gospel; then to validate the Church's extended growth in the Gentile world, under the guidance of Paul who was as Jewishly faithful and as Spirit-directed as was Peter. Luke presents the Jerusalem conference and its agreed statement (Acts 15) as an acceptable way for Gentile and Jewish Christians in his own day to respect one another and to cohere. The ending of Acts 28:16–31 must be about the year 62 CE. To Jewish leaders in Rome, aware that no one has a good word to say about this sect, Paul asserts his utter devotion to their religion, his loyalty to the hope of Israel. Some are won over, others were unconvinced. So Paul, denouncing them with words from Isaiah 6:9–10, says 'the Gentiles will listen'. For two years 'he proclaimed the Kingdom of God and taught the facts about the Lord Jesus quite openly and without hindrance'.

What then happened Luke knew but did not say. In his second book he had tacitly given up hope of mass conversion of Jews who survived in Judaea; he had provided an account of the interdependence of Jewish and Gentile Christians and a formula for their interrelation. He perhaps hoped that Domitian, the new Caesar, would now allow preaching of the Gospel 'quite openly and without hindrance'.

Chapters 1–5
After the holy period of forty days (e.g. Jesus was forty days in the wilderness (Luke 4:2), and Moses was forty days and nights on the mountain being instructed by God), during which Jesus instructed the apostles, Luke has Jesus raised into heaven where he will be seen by Stephen before his martyrdom (7:56) and, on the Damascus road, by Paul who had watched Stephen die.

The apostolic group, even though they were Galileans, remain in Jerusalem. The Christian movement, from the beginning of the story, is kept within Roman jurisdiction (which for Luke is basically helpful) and we are already looking ahead to Paul in Rome. Peter fills the vacancy left by Judas in the Twelve, which symbolically points to Israel as witnesses to the resurrection. On Pentecost (one of the three pilgrim festivals, fifty days after Passover when Jesus died), when Jerusalem was crowded with pilgrims, Jews and proselytes (i.e., converts), the Twelve had a multilingual, cross-cultural audience to hear their testimony. The Holy Spirit gave them ability and excitability to impress the crowd. From this time onwards, almost throughout Acts, the Holy Spirit is invoked as giving power to the community, as promoting boldness of speech, as prompting decisions and actions, as leading to agreement, and so on. This is illustrated by programmatic speeches (2:22–36; 3:12–26; 4:8–12 – such as could be addressed to a Jewish audience) and by programmatic sharing and disposing of property (2:44–46; 4:32–37 – such as would guide the first stages of a Jewish–Christian community). The warning story of Ananias and Sapphira in 5:1–10 is intended to say that the surrender of property is not obligatory, but if made (under the Spirit's prompting) must be genuine. The Holy Spirit's power is a communal possession, so that individual dishonesty would weaken, even destroy, the community – and its power to heal (3:1–10; 5:15–16), despite the hostility of Temple authorities, modified by Pharisaic caution (5:34–39), and by help that allowed a jail-break (5:19).

Chapters 6–7
Within the Jewish Christian community in Jerusalem, some came from a Hebraic, some from a Hellenistic background. The Greek-speaking Stephen is provoked into launching a history of Jewish disobedience to God, and he is eventually lynched by his infuriated hearers. His death (modelled on the death of Jesus) is seen by a young Jew named Saul – who came from the Hellenistic world and knew both Greek and Hebrew.

Chapters 8–15
In this section the apostles in Jerusalem have to deal with mobility of the Christian community and with hostility towards it. From Jerusalem it spreads into Judaea and the coastal plain, into Samaria and Galilee, even to Damascus (about 140 miles north-east of Jerusalem), Phoenicia (today's Lebanon) and Antioch – and from there to Cyprus and Pisidia (in the heart of modern Turkey). The romantic story in 8:26–39 hints that the Gospel was carried to the edge of the world in Ethiopia (as it was then called: now northern Sudan). Such expansion could have unforeseen results, so the Jerusalem apostles exercise a kind of oversight to make sure that admission to the community had been adequately performed – and also to distinguish the activities of the Spirit from popular magical effects. Peter himself sets out on a visitation of the coastal towns. At Caesarea, the Roman administrative capital, after an extraordinary dream about clean and unclean foods, he is confronted by a Roman officer, devoutly interested in Jewish devotion to God; and Peter perceives that the confrontation is God's doing. Peter makes one of his programmatic speeches (a very interesting one, 10:34–43). As he was speaking, 'the Holy Spirit came upon all who were listening to the message'; Peter is thereby convinced that even an uncircumcised Gentile who does not keep the food rules (though attracted to Judaism) should be baptised – and so he was. Back at Jerusalem he met objections by telling the whole story. 'This means, they said, that God has granted life-giving repentance to the Gentiles also.' 'Their doubts were silenced' – at least for the time being (11:1–18).

Among the refugee community at Antioch some members brought the message to Jews only and to no others; but some natives of Cyprus and Cyrene (North Africa) began to speak to Gentiles as well. So Jerusalem sent Barnabas (a Cypriot Jew, 4:36) to offer his support and judgement – which he shrewdly gave by recruiting Saul (now converted, but returned to his home town, Tarsus) – and in due course organising famine relief for Judaean Christians. Significantly it was taken there by Barnabas and Saul. On their return they were prompted to undertake a mission first to Cyprus, then to mainland Pisidia (chs 13–14), accomplished with no little excitement. There is a programmatic synagogue speech for Jews (13:16–41) who become hostile, and a different speech for Gentiles (14:15–17) who respond to a healing by treating the apostles as if they were pagan gods. But the definitive words are spoken by Paul (as he is now called) and Barnabas as Jerusalem spokesmen, in response to acute Jewish hostility: 'It was necessary . . . that the word of God should be declared to you first. But since you reject it and judge yourselves unworthy of eternal life, we now turn to the Gentiles' – as prefigured in Isaiah 49:6. Back at Antioch, they reported how 'God had thrown open the gates of faith to the Gentiles' (14:27).

Throughout this period, those who accepted the Gospel were Jews, Gentile converts to Judaism, devout well-wishers, and pagans. Hostility was promoted by unpersuaded Jews (foremost among them being Saul, 8:3) and some Jewish Christians; for they rightly saw a threat to their religion and their identity as God's special people. Two hundred years earlier Judaism had been bitterly divided between those who were attracted by the Greek way of life and those determined to preserve their own culture against Greek overlords determined to destroy it.

Against all probability and after immense suffering, the resisting Jews had won a victory of exhaustion. And even the later dominance of Rome (who treated the Jews as a special case) had not, despite attempts, forced Jewish religion into conformity with the Imperial cult. Why then, since Judaism was a religion worth dying for, should it be diluted by Gentile converts who lacked loyalty to the Jewish people and willingness to accept the ritual laws?

Something of that kind may have been in Saul's mind when he harried the Church (8:3), even attempting to pursue 'followers of the new way' in Damascus (9:1–2). He would understand all too well the fury of Jews after his conversion (9:23), their opposition in Pisidia (13:45, 50; 14:2, 5) and attempted murder (14:19–20). At a different level the Jerusalem apostles were in danger from King Herod Agrippa, grandson of Herod the Great, who beheaded the apostle James and arrested Peter (ch. 12). The story of Peter's escape from prison and Herod's unpleasant death is intended to indicate the significance of Peter on the Palestinian scene, and hence by comparison the importance of Paul on the eastern Mediterranean scene.

(The discomfort felt by modern readers arises less from the apparently miraculous release of Peter – the 'angel' or messenger of verses 7–8 could have been a reliable fixer – than from the callous indifference to the executed guards in verse 19.) When we come to the Jerusalem conference in chapter 15, with Paul and Barnabas under investigation, their case is supported by the leader of the apostles who had barely escaped death. By this time, however, he has been supplanted as leader of the community by James, the brother of Jesus (Gal. 1:19), who appears again in Acts 21:18–25 where he gives Paul advice that was fatally wrong.

Chapter 15 is the turning-point of Luke's account. In Jerusalem James was in charge. Peter, having made his speech, was heard and seen no more. Barnabas and Paul were listened to, commended and sent back to Antioch with firm instructions and two Jerusalem companions. After some while Paul and Barnabas, planning to revisit the Churches they had earlier founded, fell into sharp dispute about their travelling companion, and so separated: Barnabas to Cyprus, Paul to Pisidia. Everything thereafter (chs 16–28) is about the progress and fate of Paul.

But Paul's account of the dispute is far more serious. Peter visited Antioch and took his meals with Gentile Christians, until some messengers came from James. Then he drew back and began to hold aloof. So did the other Jewish Christians: 'even Barnabas was carried away and played false like the rest'. And Paul told Peter in front of the whole congregation that such conduct did not square with the truth of the Gospel. From that time, Paul ceased to be a missionary of the Church of Antioch and established his own mission Churches in the eastern Mediterranean (Gal. 2:11–14).

In Paul's account the matter in dispute at Antioch was whether Jewish Christians could take their meals with Gentile Christians who did not adopt the Jewish food laws. That might have been settled at the Jerusalem conference in Acts 15 which had been called to deal with a dispute about circumcision. In Antioch some Christians from Judaea had begun to teach 'that those who were not circumcised in accordance with Mosaic practice could not be saved' (15:1) – presumably in the forthcoming conflict between right and wrong, or even between Jews and Gentiles. Paul, Barnabas and others went to consult the apostles and elders in Jerusalem where some Christian Pharisees declared, 'Those Gentiles must be circumcised and told to keep the law of Moses.' A long debate was ended when Peter, using the example of Cornelius, insists that no unbearable yoke should be put

on the converts. James then sums up and gives his judgement
(drawing on Amos 9:11–12 in the *Greek*, not the Hebrew Bible) that
Gentile converts should be instructed by letter that they would be
acceptable if they abstained from three things: (1) food bought in the
market after it had been ritually consecrated to pagan gods; (2) marriage of near relatives (as prohibited in Leviticus 18:6–8); (3) eating
bloody meat from animals killed by strangling. (The prohibitions are
more neatly arranged when they are repeated in verse 29 and in
21:25.)

Knowing the strength of Jewish feelings, that judgement seems
generous. The demand that Gentile converts should be circumcised
is rejected. The whole burdensome scribal and Pharisaic occupation
with the Law is set aside. Only three matters that have an intimate
relation with daily family life are prohibited: the eating of food that
acknowledges the existence and power of pagan gods, the consump-
tion of blood, and unlawful sexual congress. The apostles and elders,
convinced that their decision was prompted by the Holy Spirit, put
it in a letter carried by Paul, Barnabas and two others from Jerusalem,
addressed to Antioch, capital of the united province of Syria-Cilicia.
When it was read there everybody was pleased.

So Luke says. But in Galatians 2:1–10 Paul has a different account
of a confrontation with the Jerusalem leaders (whether that particular
one or a different one scarcely matters) about the Gospel he preached
to the Gentiles and the question of circumcision. 'These men
wanted to bring us into bondage, but not for one moment did I yield
to their dictation; I was determined that the full truth of the gospel
should be maintained ... These men of repute ... imparted nothing
further to me ... The agreement was that we should go to the Gentiles,
while they went to the Jews. All they asked was that we should keep
in mind the poor' – which he did, as it turned out at the risk of his
life. When later Paul had to advise the Corinthian Church about
taking meals with their pagan neighbours (1 Cor. 8; 10:14–33) or when
he intervened in the Roman Church's disputes about eating (Rom.
14), his long and complex presentations make no mention of the
Jerusalem apostles, their decision and letter (which may have been
originally intended only for the regions mentioned in Acts 15:23).

In Galatians, it is true, Paul was writing indignantly and he may
not have fully remembered any reluctance behind the Jerusalem
decision. But he was writing twenty-five or so years before Luke, and
he had been present at the conference as Luke had not. I therefore
regard Luke's account as a proposal that might perhaps (in his own

day) hold together the Jewish and Gentile Christian communities as they move into a precarious future.

Chapters 16–20

Luke now sketches Paul's Aegean mission, beginning with Philippi and Thessalonica in Macedonia, then moving to Athens and Corinth where he spends eighteen months 'teaching the word of God' (18:11). There is a diversionary visit to Judaea and a revisiting of Churches earlier founded from Antioch; but the land route brings him to Ephesus (on the western coast of the province of Asia) where he spends more than two years speaking boldly about the Kingdom of God (19:8). Then he goes via Macedonia to Greece (i.e., Corinth) for three months, gathers round him representatives of other Churches (presumably responsible for the relief fund for the Jerusalem poor), goes north again to Philippi for Passover, and then takes the sea route to rejoin the party at Troas on his way to Jerusalem, with a brief stop at Miletus (on the coast about forty miles south of Ephesus) – and makes his farewell to the Aegean mission.

Anyone who knows the eastern Mediterranean or can use an ancient map of the region will realise that there is first-hand information in these chapters. For one thing, in 16:11–17 and 20:5–15 Luke suddenly says 'we' instead of 'they', reproducing, that is, the memory of a member of the party. So also in 21:1–18 and 27:1 – 28:16. But these passages are mostly travel information. Would that Luke had given us equally detailed information about the *Church* in Ephesus (so that we could know it as well as we know the Corinthian Church from Paul's letters)! But what he does is to show Paul performing extraordinary miracles, to tell a funny story, and to describe a public riot. In fact Luke is addressing his contemporaries and saying that opposition to the Christian religion comes either from Jews or from local trade associations; that local officials and Roman magistrates (when properly informed) are impartial or supportive; and that Paul outshone rival teachers and magicians by his miraculous powers and public oratory (e.g. his uncharacteristic address to the Areopagus council at Athens, 17:10–31). Even the final speech at Miletus, with its genuine pathos (20:18–35), shows that Luke had enormous admiration for Paul, but little understanding of his theology.

But without Luke's account of the destructive ending of Paul's ministry, setting it in relation to Jewish religion and Roman government, we ourselves would be at a loss.

Chapters 21–28

Another 'we' passage gets Paul to Jerusalem (21:1–17), where he visits James and is told that the agreement about Gentile converts (15:24–29) is still in force; but that many thousands (!) of Jewish Christians, staunch supporters of the Law, have been informed that Paul tells Jews in the Gentile world not to circumcise their children or follow the Jewish way of life. If, however, Paul will join four men taking a Nazarite vow (Num. 6:13–15), people will know that he is a practising Jew and observes the Law. How unlikely! And of course it broke down. A major riot begins (attributed to Jews from Asia – Luke is carefully not compromising Jewish Christians in the city), the Romans intervene and Paul is saved from their standard brutality by his Roman citizenship. But he is also allowed to address the crowd by telling them his conversion experience, beginning as a true-born Jew and ending as an apostle to the Gentiles (22:3–21). That again infuriates the crowd – but it displays Luke's conviction that what must be impressed on Jews is that Jesus had been seen alive after his death: the resurrection and its consequences. When Paul is brought before the Council of the Jewish people, he divides them by asserting that the dispute is about *resurrection*, approved by Pharisees, denied by Sadducees (23:6–9). When later Paul, for his protection, is taken to Caesarea and appears before the governor Felix, he says, 'In reliance on God I hold the hope, which my accusers too accept that there is to be a resurrection of good and wicked alike' (24:15). Much good it did him, for Felix (married to a Jewish woman) was a standard dilatory administrator, and kept Paul in prison for two years. His successor, Porcius Festus, proposed handing him back to Jewish authority – so Paul appealed to Caesar, as was the right of a Roman citizen (25:11). So that was that; but even so he was displayed to Agrippa II (King of the northern Palestinian territories), on a courtesy visit to the governor, in the hope that a neutral Jewish expert might explain the nature of the charges against him. So once again Paul tells his conversion story, leading to the conviction 'that the Messiah would suffer and that, as the first to rise from the dead, he would announce the dawn both to the Jewish people and to the Gentiles' (26:23). The governor thinks him mad; Agrippa says, 'In short you are trying to make me act the Christian' (which translates a famously elusive Greek sentence); but both agree that he was doing nothing deserving death or imprisonment. So Luke's message to his Gentile and Jewish readers, some time in the early 80s, is plain: the resurrection is the heart of the Gospel. It may not convert Gentile and Jewish authorities, but they will not condemn those who believe it.

What follows is a first-hand account of a sea voyage from Caesarea to Rome, at the wrong time of year for Mediterranean sailing. Paul who had three times been shipwrecked and for twenty-four hours was adrift on the open sea (2 Cor. 11:25) was the experienced and determined adviser. Luke is saying: in the disturbances of your present life, listen to Paul and be guided by him. 'And so to Rome. The Christians there had had news of us and came out to meet us . . . and when Paul saw them, he gave thanks to God and took courage' (28:14–15). He also debated with the local Jewish leaders, with only partial success. The Gentiles were more responsive. Nevertheless, 'He stayed there two full years at his own expense, with a welcome to all who came to him; he proclaimed the Kingdom of God and taught the facts about the Lord Jesus Christ quite openly and without hindrance' (28:30). So also (to hint at Luke's intention) Jewish and Gentile Christians are held within the restraints of imperial authority but, at least for a time, they can spread the Gospel openly and without hindrance.

7 Three Theological Writings

As we move on into the 80s and 90s of the first century CE we are presented with six theological writings of high quality and importance: Hebrews, Ephesians, 1 Peter, Revelation, 1 John and John's gospel.

HEBREWS

In the Authorized Version and the Revised Version of the Bible this is called 'The Epistle of Paul the Apostle to the Hebrews', thus reproducing church tradition of about the fourth century – rather earlier in the East, rather later in the West. But it is not an epistle, nor is it by Paul, and probably it was not written for Jews. In the earliest days (and ever since) who wrote it and who received it were much discussed; and we can still say no better than the great third-century scholar Origen: 'To tell the truth, only God knows.' It is more like a treatise than a letter; though chapter 13 shows that it was written for a particular community (perhaps a small household Church) whose problems were in the writer's mind. The reference to Timothy (13:23) brings the 'epistle' within the Pauline orbit but it neither claims to be by Paul, nor shows his characteristic Greek style, his method of interpreting scripture, or many of his dominant themes. Its intended readers were second-generation Christians (as appears in 2:3), familiar with a type of biblical interpretation best known to us from the first-century CE Jewish writer, Philo of Alexandria. The intended readers may have been Jewish Christians, but if they once had to repent from the deadness of their former ways and faith in God (6:1) they sound like converted Gentiles. The author's discussion of the sacrificial system is entirely based on regulations for the wilderness Tabernacle (which sometimes the author misreads), not on the actual Jerusalem Temple. By the time he writes, that Temple was destroyed – yet the scriptural instructions for sacrificial worship still existed, and had not been cancelled. So perhaps Hebrews was a searching for a re-interpretation of sacrificial worship in view of the death and resurrection of Jesus.

If so, he was developing a distinctive kind of imagery for the relation of God and heaven to the world of human beings. It may be shown by comparison with other parts of the New Testament. In the first three gospels, the living God, the creator, who alone is good and with whom all things are possible, is the Father and majestic King in the heavenly Kingdom, served by angelic messengers, who has introduced his beloved Son into the human world to deal with suffering, despair and wickedness. In John's gospel, in a similar way, God is indeed Father (but not King), the owner of a great property (John 14), with room for us all. In Paul, he is God and Father whose Son is Lord, that is, executive over a divided world and controller of heavenly energy (Spirit). In Revelation, God presides over a heavenly international court; and Jesus, as the prime victim, is given executive powers over a violently disturbed world. In Hebrews, God is indeed 'our spiritual Father' (12:9), but more importantly he is 'the Majesty in heaven' (8:1), in a heavenly sanctuary where Christ as high priest appears on our behalf (9:11, 24). The other world, of which this world is only an imperfect and unsatisfactory copy, is a temple complex – and a temple implies offerings and sacrifices.

Throughout the ancient world sacrifices dominated the relations between humanity and divinity. For example, when Paul and Barnabas cured a cripple at Lystra in Asia Minor, the people said 'The gods have come down to us in a human form' and at once prepared to offer sacrifice to them (Acts 14:8–18) – on their terms, understandably. To make such an offering shows gratitude and reverence, and thus strengthens the bond between humanity and divinity. In Judaism there were offerings of first fruits, so that the main harvest might be safely and gratefully gathered. There were libations of precious water, and of wine. There was burning of incense, in order perhaps that the trading caravans that brought the spices might be protected and prosperous. Permission to kill animals for food was acknowledged by surrendering the life-giving blood entirely and by sacrificing some part of the body or a whole animal to God. For migrating people there were sacrifices to maintain favour with the accompanying or the local deity; and for Israel there was the Passover sacrifice, commemorating their escape from slavery in Egypt and their journey to the promised land. Once there, regular daily sacrifices at the local sanctuary (and later in the Jerusalem Temple) ensured the continuation of benefits for the whole community. In normal daily life it was likely that people would unintentionally break the community rules or injure their neighbours – by accident, carelessness, ignorance or stupidity. This could be put right when offenders admitted their sin, made restitution if possible, and offered a sacrifice as a penalty. (The basic rules for remedying inadvertent sins and for refusing remedy to wilful sins are in Numbers 15:22–31.) Hence the structural importance of the daily offerings in the Temple, and the offerings at the great festivals, especially the Day of Atonement. When the Temple was destroyed in 70 CE the sacrifices ceased: the priests were killed or lost both power and function.

The gospels written after 70 CE are little interested in sacrifice; but Hebrews rethinks the scriptural interest in priesthood and sacrifice.

The writer sets out his material in formal style. First there are three basic or elementary convictions, to each of which a persuasive application is added. That done, he develops at length more mature teaching and presses it home with a substantial appeal. He ends with instructions for the community.

1:1–14
We are living in the final age when God speaks to us, not only by his usual messengers (angels) but by his incomparably greater Son.

2:1–4
Therefore we must beware of drifting from our course.

2:5–18
Jesus, however, had temporarily been made inferior to the angels because God's intention is to prepare a new world for human beings; and he is thus an intermediary between the world we live in and the world of heaven.

3:1 – 4:13
Therefore we are to think of Jesus as 'the apostle and high priest of the faith we profess', to hear *today* the warning once given to stubborn Israel, knowing that 'everything lies bare and exposed to the eyes of him to whom we must render account'.

4:14 – 5:10
Jesus as high priest has (by his resurrection) passed through the heavens and, once 'perfected', has complete and unmediated access to God who appointed him as an exclusive Melchizedek high priest. As our representative, Jesus sympathises with our weaknesses and himself 'learnt obedience through his sufferings'. Let us therefore boldly approach God for timely help.

5:11 – 6:12
Here the readers are reproved for not advancing beyond the foundation principles of their faith (interestingly listed), and indeed possibly for falling back into their former condition, whatever that was. But to encourage them to grasp the hope that is set before them, the writer decides to explain the mature teaching about Christ's Melchizedek priesthood, already mentioned.

6:13 – 10:18
The opening paragraph of Hebrews, in words from Psalm 110, says that God's Son 'took his seat at the right hand of God on high', so as to rule God's people. But as ruler he is also priest, according to the order of Melchizedek (Ps. 110:4), a name which means 'rightful king'. Only in one other place (Gen. 14:18–20) does the name Melchizedek occur, and he is a mysterious priest of God Most High, able to exact tribute from Abraham and to bless him. He was not of the tribe of Levi (which alone provided 'levitical' priests in ancient Israel); nor of course was Jesus who therefore could not literally be a priest. The Melchizedek priesthood (of which Jesus is the sole member) operates in the real, substantial world of heaven, and is therefore infinitely superior to the levitical priesthood which operates in the shadow world in which we live. Hence 'the prescribed offerings and sacrifices cannot give the worshipper a clear conscience and so bring him to perfection (i.e., complete access to God) . . . they are external ordinances in force until the coming of a new order' (9:9–10) – which is then described. The sacrificial system of Mosaic Law is only a shadow, not the real approach to the heavenly world. Jesus has entered the real sanctuary, not a copy made by human hands. He did not make repeated offerings of animal blood, but offered his own blood once and for all.

This elaborate argument (coherent too if you accept the writer's assumptions) is interested not in resurrection but in exaltation. It ends as it began by pointing (10:12–13) to Psalm 110 and then, by adding the witness of the Holy Spirit, to the new covenant promised in Jeremiah 31:33–34.

10:19 – 12:29

With splendid rhetoric and poetic fervour the writer now develops his appeal, bearing in mind the precarious (though not desperate) situation of the Church. In its earliest days its members had suffered severely and shown endurance (10:32–36), but such hardship can be regarded as discipline, and so far they had not resisted to the point of shedding their blood (12:4–13). But they were drifting off course and making no progress (2:1; 6:2), no doubt in dispirited mood. But throughout history people have lived in a problem world where survival was possible only by faith – of which there are innumerable examples (ch. 11). As the writer has already said (9:24–28), it is a shadow world, made by human hands: the real world is heaven, made by God himself. The ancient wilderness ritual provides an analogy: the outer tent was the Holy Place, and beyond the dividing curtain was the Most Holy Place (9:3). Yet that was 'but a shadow of the good things to come, not the true picture' (10:1). And now Jesus had opened for us a new and living way, having passed through the curtain of his flesh into the real world (10:20). As this appeal draws to its end, the writer varies the imagery: instead of a passage through the heavens representing an entry into the inner sanctuary, he uses the ascent of the sacred mountain to the city of the living God (12:22–29). When Christians appear before him for judgement, the blood of Abel does not accuse them but the blood of Jesus pleads for them, that they may indeed worship, with reverence and awe, the God who is a devouring fire.

Chapter 13

Most of these community instructions are sensible and straight-forward. Verse 10 may imply that Christians have an altar in the heavenly world where Christ is our high priest, whereas the altar once served by the Jewish priesthood has been destroyed. The final blessing in verses 20–21 looks like a traditional prayer mentioning Christ's resurrection (not elsewhere in Hebrews), slightly modified by 'the blood of the eternal covenant' which echoes the dominant theme of chapters 9 and 10.

EPHESIANS

Like Hebrews, this letter is interested in the heavenly realms and in the Church's origin in Jewish religious life. Indeed, it was probably written to draw together Jewish and Gentile Christians when they were threatened not so much by the hostility of neighbours and government but by the assumptions and prejudices that unquestionably dominated life in the Empire (6:12). The letter is ascribed to Paul (writing from prison), but it differs greatly from other Pauline letters. Such matters are best dealt with after it has been read and considered.

1:1–2
This looks like the standard beginning of a Pauline letter (such as 2 Corinthians) sent 'to God's people who are in Ephesus and faithful in Christ Jesus'. But the earliest Greek manuscripts of this letter indicate no destination – the words 'in Ephesus' are not present – and that fact was known to Origen in the third century and to Basil in the fourth. This therefore looks like a general letter, since it deals with no particular problems and sends greetings to no named persons.

1:3–14
This is a blessing of God, the Hebrew form of thanksgiving. In Greek it is one complex sentence, so that whatever is said is linked with and dependent on everything else that is said. Nothing can be preferred, nothing set aside. The heavenly realms are more important than the world, but it is God's secret purpose that 'everything in heaven and earth might be brought into unity in Christ'. God acts always in Christ, choosing us, predestining us, securing our release, and so on – where 'us' at first means Jewish Christians and then is extended to Gentile Christians: 'you also'.

1:15–23
Thanksgiving now becomes petition for Gentile Christians that they may realise how rich and glorious is what God offers. It is, literally, life from the dead and enthronement above all government and authority, in the present age and the coming age. The means of God's dominance over space and time is the Church, of which Christ is head.

2:1–10

This rephrases what has just been said, namely that we have been brought from death to life in Christ Jesus, but it agrees that Jews were in no better state than Gentiles and concedes that their new life resulted not from their own improvement but from God's grace.

2:11–22

Gentile Christians are reminded of the Jewish view of pagan society: totally alienated from the true God and his promises. But the blood of Christ has replaced the blood of circumcision, the barrier of the Law has been removed, a new humanity has overcome the enmity, and Gentiles are no longer aliens but members of God's household. Jews and Gentiles together constitute a temple built upon apostles and (Christian) prophets with Jesus Christ as the cornerstone (or possibly keystone).

3:1–13

This begins as a prayer for Gentile Christians, and so continues in verses 14–19, with a doxology in verses 20–21. But it is interrupted in verses 2–13 by the need to admit that Paul writes from prison, and to justify his sufferings. In fact, when this letter was in circulation Paul was dead and had been replaced by Christ's 'holy apostles and prophets' (v. 5).

4:1 – 6:9

The rest of the letter is an encouragement to replace pagan behaviour by Christian (the usual middle section of a Pauline letter is missing). There is emphasis both on the unity given by the Spirit and the variety of gifts, an appeal to 'give up living as pagans do', and a set of rules for the Christian household (as in Colossians) based on submission, like some kinds of Hellenistic morality. These rules have already appeared in Colossians 3:18 – 4:1. They will reappear, more elaborately, in 1 Peter 2:11 – 3:7 and Titus 2:1–10. They demonstrate Christians accommodating themselves to a society which they seem unlikely to transform. Submission may be a more effective influence than hostility. Verse 21 requires mutual submission within the community: there are to be no overbearing Church leaders. What follows is a reasonably sensitive attempt to remodel pagan rules in a Christian style. Since Christ is the head of the Church (i.e., its promoter and leader) and its self-sacrificing saviour, so husbands must love their wives, and wives must allow their husbands so to behave. It is an interesting attempt to make a jigsaw of Christian and pagan responses; but it is deeply unsatisfactory, even if we overlook Christian ownership of slaves (6:9). Slaves are to 'give single-minded obedience to their earthly masters with fear and trembling – as if to Christ' (6:5). But what if slave-masters were intent on sexual male abuse? We must realise that the writer of Ephesians was making the best he could of rules that were unsatisfactory then and are more unsatisfactory now.

6:10–23
The conclusion offers a flamboyant icon of the well-armed Christian soldier (whose only weapon is the word of God), a request for constant prayer, two verses lifted out of Colossians 4:7–8, and a benediction.

Now we may consider authorship. Since the author is in prison, this 'letter' seems close to Colossians, of which it makes much use, though treating important words in a novel way. The standard middle section of a Pauline letter (dealing with a religious problem) is missing, so that the author produces theological reflection without the stimulus of a precise theological need. It is written to no particular community and the readers are all-purpose Gentiles, once morally disreputable, now needing encouragement not to fall back into old habits. It is written at a time when Paul had been succeeded by the holy apostles and prophets, as a general instruction to Gentile Christians, with the intention of saying: these are the consequences and meaning of what Paul taught *then* in the situation we have *now*.

1 PETER
This letter, like Ephesians which the writer may have known and quoted, is another general instruction. It was addressed to Christians in the great area north and west of the Taurus mountains (i.e., the bulk of modern Turkey) which earlier had been part of Paul's mission field. It is written in excellent Greek (better than Paul's), quotes extensively from the Old Testament, and uses Jewish references and ideas to support mainly Gentile Christian communities (1:14, 18; 2:10; 3:6; 4:3). If it is right to place this letter after Ephesians in the reign of Domitian, then perhaps it was an attempt by the Petrine mission to strengthen part of the Pauline community that was in danger of collapse. But that can be considered later.

1:1–2

This opening greeting provides the key to the whole letter: its readers, by their religion, are aliens and exiles. They have responded to God's foreknowledge (1:3–12), have been made God's people by the Holy Spirit (1:13 – 2:10), and in their obedience share Christ's sufferings (2:11 – 4:11).

1:3–12

Aliens have a precarious existence, but Christians who have 'dropped out' of pagan society are sustained by hope (as powerful a word as 'faith' in this letter). Hope is modelled on death and resurrection (or new birth) and on the conviction that the present time is coming to an end.

1:13 – 2:10

Since the Holy Spirit is the life-giver, death and resurrection are presented in various metaphors – rebirth, the stone rejected and then prized, the change from darkness to light, the conversion of non-people to God's people – together with the moral consequences.

2:11 – 4:11

For aliens and exiles the proper functioning and reputation of the family is important, hence this section on good behaviour and submission to the authorities, with special paragraphs on slaves and masters (2:18–25), wives and husbands (3:1–7). Christian submission has already been considered in dealing with Ephesians 5:21 – 6:9. It is perhaps more understandable here since the readers need help in their anxiety. At all points the sufferings of Christ have a bearing on present or possible Christian sufferings; and by an imaginative use of Noah's flood, baptism is shown to encourage those who suffer and even die (3:18–22). Despite hardships, the readers have changed from the dissipation of paganism to Christianity – from death to life – and, since the end of all things is near, they must practise family love (4:1–11).

4:12 – 5:11

Once more the writer offers pastoral advice for dealing with what these 'aliens' are possibly suffering (in 1:6 and 3:13, 17 where the language is tentative), though at least some of them have now endured suffering as a fiery testing (like the testing of precious metals as in 1:7 – 'ordeal' may be an over-reaction to the wording in 4:12).

They may even suffer simply because they are Christians (4:16). That kind of thing is happening to fellow Christians in all the world (5:9). But they must not attract hostility by criminal or unsocial behaviour (4:15), and the elders have a special responsibility for the flock of God.

5:12–14

The authority behind this letter is Peter or the continuing Petrine mission. The actual writer is Silvanus who joins Mark in sending greetings from Babylon (a code-name, in Jewish writings of this period, for Rome). Silvanus brings to mind a former associate of Paul (in Thessalonians and 2 Corinthians), probably the same as Silas in Acts 16 – 18. Mark had contacts with both Peter and Paul. Hence this final greeting indicates that the Christian Church in Rome, backed by associates of Peter and Paul, is doing what it can to encourage hard-pressed communities in the former Pauline mission area. It is necessary to put the letter at a date after Peter's death because, first, the writer knows Ephesians; second, the quality of the Greek is beyond a bilingual Jewish fisherman; and, third, the risk of persecution in Asia Minor for bearing the name of Christian is not earlier than the reign of Domitian.

8 The School of John

REVELATION

For some, Revelation (not 'Revelations' as people persistently miscall it) is the most fascinating, for others the most exasperating book in the New Testament. It belongs to a style of writing called 'apocalyptic'. Specimens have already turned up in Paul's letters (1 Thess. 4:15–17; 2 Thess. 2:1–12; 1 Cor. 15:20–28) and in Mark 13. In this first-century period, Jewish writers were producing major examples (such as the apocalypses of 1 Enoch, 4 Ezra and 2 Baruch), all of which look back to the visions of Daniel. 'Apocalyptic' seems like a technical term, but it is no more than a simple Greek word. *Calymma* is a veil or cover. *Calypsis* is a veiling, and *Apocalypsis* is an unveiling. In apocalyptic writings the author purports to uncover what is really going on in his changing world. As far as his eye can see, society has moved into an unstable situation with natural disaster and human wickedness on a massive scale, something far more alarming than the familiar struggles between rival groups and expected changes of climate. So there are prophetic writers (they discern what is happening but do not necessarily forecast what *will* happen) who portray the violent engagement of superpowers in the imagery available to them.

To modern readers much of the imagery seems grotesque and unpleasant, so it is worthwhile considering why it is as it is.

Two thousand years ago, human beings had very little physical power unless they acted (or were made to act) together in vast throngs. But they were constantly under threat from the power of natural forces. As the imagery indicates there were clouds and winds, thunder, lightning, hailstorms, floods, torrents, scorching heat, and meteorites. There were earthquakes and volcanoes; with fire and sulphurous smoke (as anybody knows who has been to Naples and Vesuvius – which exploded in 79 CE). There were plagues, pestilence, famine, disaster, warfare, massacres, bereavement, death and Hades. That story of everyday life in the Mediterranean is qualified by the extraordinary survival and physical powers of lions, oxen, eagles, horses, sea monsters, scorpions and locusts. Horses and oxen can be domesticated, but the rest cannot – and they may be dangerous. It is not surprising that the grotesque and terrifying beast in this book is symbolic of ruthless imperial government, and that 'Satan' refers to the demand that the Emperor should be addressed in Asia Minor (the centre of the emperor cult) as 'my Lord and my God'. In complete contrast, of course, there are agents and messengers of God who need no symbolic guise: the spirits and angels who appear some seventy times in this Apocalypse. And even the disturbed and disturbing natural world can provide gentle symbols: as when the floods and torrents become the river of the water of life; as when the terrifying beasts are replaced by the Lamb that was slain.

1:1–3
Most apocalypses are supposedly written by prominent people of the past, such as Enoch, Ezra and Baruch (mentioned above). But this one is written by John who had responsibility for seven Churches in the province of Asia. He was a Jewish Christian prophet who received his inspiration in symbolic visions, but he was not an apostle (and therefore not John Zebedee) since he speaks of the twelve apostles as other than himself (18:20; 21:14). Despite traditions from the early Church (which say that he wrote in the reign of Domitian) he was not the author of the fourth gospel. This John wrote in a peculiarly fractured Greek (possibly deliberately), quite different from the simple but lucid Greek of the gospel. His obsessive concern with the forthcoming end of this epoch has almost no place in the gospel, and the gospel's profound retelling of the earthly life of Jesus has no place in the Apocalypse. Its writer is not prophesying about the remote future but about 'what must soon take place . . . for the time of fulfilment is near' – as he says again at the end (22:10).

1:4–20
Nominally this is a pastoral letter to 'seven churches in the province of Asia', named in the order that a traveller might visit them, starting from Ephesus as centre and walking a semi-circle of a hundred-mile radius. The writer had been (perhaps as punishment) on Patmos, a small, rocky island in the Sporades group, not far from Ephesus (1:9). The letter begins formally with greetings from God (the existent Being

who is master of past and future), from the fullness of spiritual energy
('seven' is an indicator of totality), and from the risen Christ who
claims allegiance and obedience from ruling authorities. Then comes
the first of many doxologies, insisting that the death of Christ has
both set Christians free from the disabling consequences of their sins
and also made them priests (who show God to the world and show
the world how to honour God). Verse 7 now tells us what the theme
of the Apocalypse will be: the coming of God with the clouds and
the consequent repentance of all peoples of the world. To understand
'coming with the clouds', think what clouds imply in the Near East:
relief and shade from extreme heat, possibly rain after drought,
perhaps devastating storms and flooding – all beyond human control.
Finally the Lord God says 'I am the Alpha and Omega' – the first
and last letters of the Greek alphabet. Not the Hebrew Aleph and
Tau, because the writer is transferring the Jewish dependence on
written *scripture* to the Greek-speaking Church. From beginning to
end, what is important is the written word of God. The verb *write*
comes twenty-seven times in the Apocalypse, beginning with verse 3
and continuing with verse 11.

It is important to know that, in the ancient world, reading was
reading aloud. So John's imagery was intended for the ear, not the
eye. Neither in vision nor in imagination did he actually *see* anything.
He was using the common Hebraic way of expressing ideas without
resorting to abstract language. When he says 'I saw' he means 'I
perceived'. If modern western readers try to draw pictures of what
John describes, the results are grotesque and incompatible. We must
learn the skill of translating the pictorial language into its reasonable
equivalent – without losing too much of its imaginative vigour. That,
of course, is what John himself expects us to do (with hints in verse
20).

In the forefront of this passage he puts alarm about death and
Hades: the 'power to kill by sword and famine, by pestilence and wild
beasts' (6:8). On the Lord's Day – the day of resurrection – he perceives
the immense majesty of one who holds the keys of death and Hades.
He is dressed (with his long robe and breast girdle) like a person of
high rank; his hair indicates great age and experience; his gaze is
penetrating; his stance is immovable; his voice drowns all opposition.
When he speaks he can slay; when he looks at you it is like the sun
in full strength. (Most of this imagery comes from Daniel and Ezekiel.)
This is the Lord Jesus Christ in the midst of his Churches (which are
places of illumination), holding in his hand seven stars which,

however, are God's messengers to the Churches. Astrology is replaced by direct reliance on the grasp of Christ.

Chapters 2–3
The seven Churches are individually assessed, rebuked and commended. There is a brooding unease, but only one martyr is named (2:13).

Chapters 4–5
The world as John knows it is a place of suffering, terror and death – for individuals and communities. Can the divine justice stop the evil, restore its victims, and produce a new world? He begins with the royal throne in an eastern throne-room which soon becomes a courtroom. Modern readers must realise that ancient oriental sovereignty and judiciary are quite unlike modern practice, and we must use our imaginative abilities to grasp what is going on.

The enthroned Being is like jasper or cornelian (permanent colours, not fading in the Mediterranean sunshine), surrounded by a planetary halo of brilliant green (a symbol of young, new life). Encircling the throne are twenty-four elders, who represent community tradition and often initiate the praise of God, so that justice and worship are joined. There are representations of the divine powers: lightning and thunder, flaming torches (the investigative spirits), the turbulence of the sea under control, and the four sources of living energy: lion, ox, human and eagle. That remarkable assembly now operates as a royal court. A sealed scroll is produced, written on both sides, that is, packed with pleas and criminal charges that are to be presented to the royal Being. But who will present them? Not the Lion from the tribe of Judah (by now compromised and discredited), but the sacrificed Lamb. The indictment is made not by a political power-broker but by a victim. This presents Jesus as an unblemished person, wholly devoted in sacrifice to God, fully empowered (seven horns) and fully informed (seven eyes) to put the case for suffering humanity.

6:1 – 8:1
The seals are broken, displaying (1) aggression and domination; (2) war and slaughter; (3) scarcity of food and manipulation of markets; (4) policies that ruin a quarter of the population; (5) martyrdom; and (6) damage to the very fabric of the world and panic at the highest levels. In chapter 7 victims get the protection of the court, and at 8:1 the court takes a recession.

8:2 – 11:19

The court reconvenes, with the aim of calling the people to repentance. (That is the meaning of the trumpets – see Joel 2, especially verses 15–17.) All in response to the prayers of God's people (8:3–5). They are to repent that: a third of the earth was ruined and made unproductive; a third of the sea was devastated by volcanic eruption and tidal wave; a third of water supplies were polluted; and a third of the sky was obliterated – disastrous consequences of human wickedness and disrespect for the universe. Hence the vulture (rather than 'eagle') in 8:13.

When the fifth trumpet sounds the pressure is increased: human disrespect for the universe is not only hugely damaging but (with volcanic eruptions supplying the imagery) destructive of the world's foundations. This is disaster ('woe' in 9:12 is too feeble), causing not only acute suffering but also terror as well as mental ruin. Hence the fantastical invasion of locusts, and (with the sixth trumpet) 200 million grotesque cavalry. Yet these warnings did nothing to persuade people to abandon idolatry or to repent their wickedness.

So it would seem necessary to try again – with the seven thunders, the veritable voice of God. But no! What God says is to be sealed up, not written down. The procedure of the heavenly court is revised: there is to be no more delay. John himself must eat the little scroll – 'little' because it is an indictment he can deal with – and he will find it to his liking but to his disadvantage. That is, once again he must utter prophecies over many nations, races, languages and kings (10:11).

11:1–13

This sections sets out such a programme. To anyone unfamiliar with prophecy, it is strange indeed. You have to keep in mind that prophecy, looking towards the future, demands 'an imaginative response. It sets in motion stored memories, calls upon remembered scripture, and relives recent events, anxieties and hopes. What John and his readers have in mind is the recent destruction, by the Roman army, of Jerusalem and the Temple, and the killing by the Roman Emperor of Peter and Paul. What then can be said, perhaps in veiled language, about the foreseeable future? The prophecy is dominated by three-and-a-half years or days (it comes from 'time, two times, and half a time' in Daniel 12:7), implying 'in the short term', since seven is the totality symbol.

It will be sensible to take this verse by verse.

The prophet must first measure the temple of God (an image from Ezek. 40–48) and count the worshippers. That is the protected area, and they are the protected people. Whatever imperial Rome can do, the essential existence of the Christian Church (unlike the Jerusalem Temple) is safe (v. 1). But the outer court cannot claim protection: in the actual world of Roman domination, Christians will be oppressed (v. 2). But even there they will have powerful and effective witnesses to the truth, dressed in sackcloth as a signal for repentance (Jonah 3:6, 8) (v. 3). Such witnesses are part of Israel's historical experience, like the two olive trees and the two lamps (suggesting healing and illumination) in Zechariah 4:3 (v. 4), whose fiery words damage and destroy their enemies (v. 5); or like Elijah (1 Kings 17:1) and Moses (Exod. 7:14–15) (v. 6). Yet even such witnesses, like Peter and Paul, will not survive attack by the abysmal beast (the Roman imperial power) (v. 7), or the contempt of pagan enemies (vv. 8–10). But after death comes resurrection and ascent to God in heaven (vv. 11–12), while on earth the second disaster horrifies all, kills 7,000, and at last prompts repentance by the survivors (vv. 13–14). The seventh trumpet sounds: to the assessors in the heavenly court this seems like a triumphant conclusion. But not so: there are more serious things to come (v. 15).

12:1–17

To many readers of the Apocalypse it seems that the writer is needlessly prolonging his account of distress and disaster, sometimes bluntly stated, sometimes fancifully described. But so to judge him is to misunderstand his intention. We who have lived during the twentieth century can surely not be insensitive to the dreadful things that have happened, are happening, and will get worse. We can hear firsthand news reports, see appalling pictures, feel helpless before the statistics – and panic begins to edge its way in as we wonder what kind of universe it is we now live in. So it is with John: his concern is no longer the conflict between a secure heaven and a world that is ruining itself. The conflict seems to be with heaven itself (vv. 7–12).

It is indeed true that the whole universe is always under threat from powerful hostile forces (indicated by the traditional imagery of 'the great dragon, the ancient serpent'). Even in heaven there is malicious opposition to God's people from the Devil (meaning 'slanderer') or Satan (meaning 'adversary' as in Job 2). This opposition is in conflict with their protector Michael (Dan. 12) and his angels, who are symbols of God's wholly personal care for his people. But the battle is already won by the sacrifice of the Lamb and the martyrdom of Christians; and the hostile powers are driven from heaven to earth. This dramatic imagery implies that the Roman imperial power has lost any divine sanction it may once have had (as, for example, in Romans 13). This is no longer a world (shall we say?) in which people take it for granted that of course the Divine Will expects disobedient slaves to be crucified.

But on earth there is still hostility between the Roman imperium and the Church. Indeed this is the third woe or disaster (v. 12), described in words that recall the volcanic disaster – implying that the Roman imperium is as terrifying and damaging as a natural explosion. The earthly story, told in the language of myth, begins in verses 1–6 and 13–17. In the intention of heaven, the Woman is more important for human existence than the celestial objects, than sun, moon and stars of the zodiac. (Observe, by the way, the fundamental significance of this feminine image.) She is the glorified Israel, the bride of God, and (to Christians) the Church. And Israel is in distress until Messiah is born (v. 2), because it is confronted with the Mediterranean superpower, the 'volcanic' fiery dragon (vv. 3 and 4). Nothing is said in verse 5 about Messiah's life and death because the Apocalypse is presenting Jesus as an officer of the heavenly court (5:6–7). But the Woman – now perceived as the Church – has to take refuge in the wilderness (i.e., the Church is marginalised) where Rome's powers might not reach – apart from the undiscriminating tidal wave (v. 15).

13:1–10
The dragon 'took his stand on the sea shore' – which allows John to redouble his myth-making activity. Here is an immense maritime power, unlike anything else, totally inhuman. Even if one of its leaders had seemingly been given a death blow, it could recover – to the whole world's wondering admiration. It was given 'authority over every tribe, nation, language and race', even claiming allegiance due only to God, and 'allowed to wage war on God's people and to defeat them'. How could this ruthless and blasphemous empire attract so much approval? Because the names of the empire's supporters were not 'written from the foundation of the world in the book of life of the Lamb that was slaughtered' – which is the NRSV translation, in line with a similar phrase in 17:8. The writer means that those who accept the Lamb's example of death and resurrection will survive in

this world, and 'this calls for the endurance and faithfulness of God's people'.

13:11–18

The danger is all the greater because the Roman imperium is a delusive parody of true devotion. A beast from the earth with two horns like a lamb's (a parody of the Lamb of God), but which spoke like a dragon (a parody of the voice of God), made people worship the beast whose mortal wound had been healed (a parody of the resurrection), made fire come down to earth (a parody of Pentecost) – and so on. This denunciation ends with the numbers game whereby letters of the Greek or Hebrew alphabets are given numbers (alpha = 1, beta = 2, and so on). Any Christian would know that the number of Jesus in Greek is 888. The number of the beast is 666, as much inferior to the wholeness of 777 as 888 exceeds it.

Everything in chapter 13 could have been meaningful and seriously intended for the first readers of the Apocalypse. There is no need for modern readers to puzzle overmuch about the details of such ancient ingenuity.

Chapter 14

Chapter 14 is the beginning of the end, so it is helpful to review the course so far. In chapter 6–7 the breaking of the seven *seals* displayed the indictment of the pagan world, and relief was promised for 144,000 from the tribes of Israel and for an uncountable number from all races. In chapters 8–9 the seven *trumpets* were a persistent call to repentance, though with little response. So in chapter 10 the seven *thunders* followed – but were not written down. Instead John was to prophesy against the Roman beast (ch. 11) producing acute hostility between the Empire and the Church (chs 12–13). Now in chapter 14 the fight-back begins.

14:1–5

We return to the scene of chapter 4. We see mount Zion, the heavenly Jerusalem – with the Throne, the Lamb, the four living creatures and twenty-four Elders. They sing a new song (as in 5:9) that can be learnt only by the 144,000 (first presented in 7:4–8) who are the first-fruits of humankind. They follow the Lamb wherever he goes (including death and resurrection) and they are virgins 'who have not defiled themselves with women'.

We must pause for a moment to consider that phrase. Some people are so shocked by it that they cannot work out its implications. Jewish writers were not shocked by sexual activity or imagery (look at the Song of Songs, attributed to Solomon). Nor was the writer of the Apocalypse, to judge by the bride and bridegroom imagery in his final chapters. But it was the rule that men fighting in a holy war must abstain from sex (Deut. 23:9–10); 'being defiled' means not being in condition to perform holy duties. Therefore John's 144,000 are young unmarried men, likely to die, and incapable of continuing their families – martyrs in several respects.

14:6–13
Officers of the heavenly court (six angels) now briskly initiate the next stage. Angel 1 announces an eternal gospel for every community of people, and bids them submit to God's decisions as creator. Angel 2 announces the fall of Babylon (Isa. 21:9); that is, the judgement goes against the corrupt city civilisations of the Near East. Angel 3 gives the verdict on those who are wholly devoted to the Empire: they will experience God's wrath and anger with no respite day or night, that is, they will be punished by the dreadful consequences of their own obsessive wickedness – from which God will no longer protect them. Provided, that is, that God's people remain constant – for there will indeed be respite for those who die in the faith.

14:14–20
So much for decisions. Now actions are planned, using harvest language. The 'figure like a man' of 1:3 now appears on a white cloud (as promised in 1:7) with 'a sharp sickle in his hand'. Angel 4 announces and reaps the grain harvest, the safe gathering-in of God's people. Angel 5 with a sharp sickle is prompted by Angel 6 (in charge of the altar fire) to gather the ripe grape harvest – in the spirit of Joel 3:13. But who harvests grapes with a sickle, and why is fire necessary? In the Apocalypse, wine is (a) the product of the disreputable commercial world (6:6; 18:13) and a symbol of peoples' faithlessness (17:2); and (b) a symbol of God's disapproval and anger (14:8, 10, 19, 20; 16:19; 18:3; 19:15). Therefore the crop is to be destroyed and the vines burnt. This imagery and its gruesome application comes from Isaiah 63:3–6, but it is becoming rather overloaded. In verse 20, 'outside the city' may imply the crucifixion and suggest extensive martyrdom – the 'two hundred miles' perhaps referring to the whole length of Palestine or of Italy.

Chapters 15–16

We now move towards the last phase of God's destructive anger. It begins with a triumph song of those who had faithfully resisted the Beast (15:2–4), and then introduces angels with their seven bowls and torments: the last torments of all – for when a bowl is empty it is empty. And for good reason: human societies are incapable – by themselves alone – of repenting for what they have done or of turning to God for help. The first four bowls totally damage earth, sea, rivers and sun. The last three injure the heathen Empire, the battle-array of conspiring kings, and (with another volcano) the solid world itself. 'Armageddon', by the way, means hill or mountain of Megiddo, but Megiddo is on low, flat ground – as a glance at the Israel Survey proves. John is working towards a Grand Grand-Finale, beginning in 16:19–21. The bowl angels have other duties as well: in 17:1 one of them shows the verdict on the Empire and in 21:10 another shows the renewed Church.

Chapters 17–18

The responsibility for these disasters is now placed insistently but obscurely on the great whore and her foul fornication. In the Hebrew Bible, 'fornication' can be a metaphor for unfaithfulness to God or for ruthless commercial exploitation (for example in the ruin of Sidon and Tyre in Isaiah 23 and the laments over Tyre in Ezekiel 26 – 27). That is the meaning here (18:3). If, a little more generally, we ask ourselves what is wrong with fornication – putting aside the stock answers – the reply might be that in prostitution all creative energy and nurturing ability goes into pleasurable excitement, often to the careless and cruel satisfaction of the powerful. John's disapproving sexual language is condemning a ruthless and irresponsible kind of social existence.

Rome, in its way reproducing the domination of ancient Babylon, is presented as a powerful maritime and trading power – with enormous wealth and display. In John's imagery it appears as the goddess Roma seated upon a scarlet beast (red being a favourite Roman colour). This identification becomes clear in the seven hills on which Rome is built (17:9, and 'the great city' in verse 18). The seven kings – or perhaps eight in verses 10–11 – are a nominal roll call of emperors; though from our modern knowledge of Roman history it is not possible to discover precisely what John had in mind. Nor does it matter. The ten kings in verse 12 are barbaric forces from beyond the Empire (the 'Kings from the east' of 16:12) who 'will come to hate the whore'.

John is saying that the Empire which seems so powerful and enduring, so hostile to Christians, will in fact be destroyed.

So in chapter 18 there is a magnificent taunt-song against the commercial basis of this Empire, not celebrating its destruction but intending to provoke it. The list of commodities, true to the historical evidence, ends with 'slaves, and human lives' (v. 13), and the punishment of the Empire is to endure the consequences of what it was doing (vv. 6 and 23).

19:1–10

The Heavenly Court celebrates the expected end of the Empire and looks forward to a replacement Kingdom, to be inaugurated on earth by the marriage of the Lamb (21:2). His bride will be God's people, wearing fine linen – which signifies their righteous deeds. Thus the corrupt behaviour of the Empire is to be replaced by the proper behaviour of Christians – if, that is, they are serious in accepting their invitation to the wedding breakfast of the Lamb.

19:11 – 20:3

The destruction of the Empire will take place not simply by the collapse of a merchandise economy, but 'the Lamb will conquer them for he is Lord of lords and King of kings and those who are with him are called and chosen and faithful' (17:14). The slain Lamb of 5:6 acts on behalf of all victims. He treads the winepress (14:20) and comes as the avenger of blood (6:10; 19:2), now 'in a garment dyed in blood and riding a white horse, followed by 'the armies of heaven', that is, the faithful of chapters 7 and 14.

This talk of vengeance does not imply vindictiveness: it implies that the social order ruptured by the crime is to be restored, that the victim is justly satisfied, and that the offender is required to experience the victim's hurt.

Not of course that John is predicting and desiring actual slaughter, but he knows that the powerful do not voluntarily give up power. Hence his savage imagery of a gruesome feast (which he borrows from Ezekiel 39) with the vultures performing their useful cleansing operation. The immense power structure of the Empire is destroyed: 'the flesh of Kings, commanders, and warriors, the flesh of horses and their riders, the flesh of all, the free and the slave' is consumed – and the Mediterranean lands are left clean. But what will replace the Empire? Some other power structure will necessarily be built – and how can it be protected from the growth and dominance of a new form of 'emperor worship'? There is a constant feature of human societies – John names it Satan or the Devil – that sooner or later will demand a total allegiance that is proper only to God. John can conceive it possible that Satan or the Devil could be chained up for a thousand years 'so that he might not seduce the nations again' – but not more than that.

20:4–10

Now that John has got rid of the Roman Empire – at least in imagination – he has to discover what happens next. Indeed, what will happen in the next thousand years? Not surprisingly his answer is elusive, but he seems to mean that Christians will be in control, supported and ministered to by the faithful martyrs now restored to life (people who would rather die than deny the truth), and under the sovereignty of Christ who is both the slain Lamb (the Victim) and the Faithful and True rider on the white horse (the Avenger). This initiates the first resurrection, when the world remains the same but new life is given to the recently dead.

But John knows too much about the Churches of Asia (remember the letters in chapters 2 and 3) to suppose that an Empire run by Christians could in the long run be free from corruption, violence and injustice. The diabolic influences that beset the Empire would seductively reappear and do their damage (Gog and Magog come from Ezekiel 38 – 39, in an earlier prophetic attempt to describe the recovery and perils of God's people). They would indeed be overcome (like the beast and the false prophet) by the cleansing power of holy fire but would never become wholly dormant (which is the implication of 'tormented day and night forever').

20:11–15

In effect, John is saying that you can try for a thousand years, but the present world will never be what it ought to be. It cannot be reformed – only destroyed. But it is God's creation: only he can end it, save what must be saved, and replace it with a new creation. John sees a great white throne (remember 4:2). For us thrones are merely ceremonial or publicity accessories, but for the Apocalypse (which uses the word twice as often as all the rest of the New Testament) 'throne' initiates the conflict between Divine Being and Satan (i.e., the Empire, 2:13; 13:2; 16:10). 'Throne' signifies power that is ultimate and immensely varied; applied in the past, the present and all the future. It commands immense approval and adoration for its protection against cruel hostility; and possesses stored information (books that must be consulted, interpreted and acted upon). This enthronement power is shared with the Lamb who is both Victim and Avenger (3:21; 5:6–7; 6:16–17).

From the presence of the Enthroned Being the whole structure of both heaven and earth vanished (as in Ps. 102:25–27) and only human beings are left. Death and Hades and the Sea release their captives: what they have done is on record. Entry in the book of life depends not on family, language or Empire, not on being great and small, but on each person's deeds. Death and Hades are flung into the lake of fire, so also are those not written in the book of life, and the sea is also destroyed (21:1). This is the second death from which there is no continuing life and no resurrection, that is, the destructive forces are really destroyed. They will not spring into life again.

21:1 – 22:5

There is to be 'a new heaven and a new earth': no longer God in heaven and the people of God on earth, but God dwelling in the midst of his people. Hence no temple is needed because God and the Lamb are there. God's people need two things: a loving relation to God (hence the marriage of the Lamb, taking up reconciliation themes from Hosea) and illumination (hence there is no night, for the glory of God gives light, as in Isaiah 60). The Holy City has been entirely reconstructed (as promised in Isaiah 65:17–25) and it is now an enormous cube (its edge is 1,500 miles long) with twelve gates and foundations of precious stones. The implications of this apparently grotesque imagery are, however, clear: the heavenly world of God's people is huge (entirely capable of admitting all who belong and ought to be there); it stands four-square and is impregnable (unlike Jerusalem in 70 CE); its structure and construction are colourful and unfading (i.e., the precious stones); it is open to all, but excludes everything vile and repulsive; and admission is by understanding and accepting the apostolic teaching. Its citizens are not indifferent to the needs of others who live on the new earth, but 'by its light shall the nations walk' and the leaves of the trees (on either side of the central river of the water of life) 'are for the healing of the nations'.

22:6–21

In this final section, John asserts the truth of his Apocalypse, thanks his angelic informant, tells readers to take it as it is (adding and subtracting nothing), and stresses its immediate significance. As he said at the beginning and warned the Asian Churches (1:1; 2:16; 3:11) this is to happen *soon* – so in verses 7, 12, 20, 'The words of the prophecy that are in this book ... the time of fulfilment is near' (v. 10). 'Come!' say the Spirit and the bride. 'Come! let each hearer reply' (v. 17). 'Amen, Come, Lord Jesus' (v. 20). Which recalls how that was said in the earliest Aramaic-speaking Church '*marana tha*' (1 Cor. 16:22) and could indeed be said at the Lord's Supper (1 Cor. 11:26). The Apocalypse is not a long-deferred programme for overthrowing an empire at a remote future time, but a programme for exposing and resisting political-merchantile regimes whenever there are Christians to utter and suffer.

THE GOSPEL AND LETTERS OF JOHN

Five New Testament writings are associated with the name of John. The author of Revelation gives his own name and distinguishes himself from the twelve apostles. He was certainly not the composer of the gospel or of any of the letters since his style of Greek and manner of expressing himself are wholly different. He wrote for the Churches of the province of Asia, and there is a fairly early but not fully persuasive tradition that the gospel too was written by the apostle John in Ephesus. But Antioch and Alexandria have been plausibly suggested as great cities where the style and subject matter of the gospel could have been developed. The final (perhaps supplementary) chapter of the gospel mentions the disciple whom Jesus loved 'who vouches for what has been written here', but it is not clear whether that means the particular episode, or the final chapter, or the whole gospel. The three Johannine letters obviously belong to the same religious world as the gospel. The Second and Third Letters are written by the Elder (or presbyter): they are genuine letters, one to a congregation, the other to an individual. The First Letter is by a known but unnamed person (who does not call himself 'the Elder'), writing not a letter but an instruction booklet, indicating to travelling preachers how to deal with problems in the Johannine group of Churches.

2 AND 3 JOHN

The Second Letter is written to a Christian community, personified as a Lady chosen by God and her children (since *ecclesia* is feminine in Greek). The writer calls himself 'the Elder' (or presbyter), who plans to visit them and sends greetings from a sister community. He explains that loving one another means living by the commands of God (whatever they are), and he warns them against people who have left the community, who are opposed to Christ in the flesh and want to go beyond his teaching. Such people are not to be admitted or listened to.

This indicates an impediment to loving, an uncertainty or disagreement about the commands of God, and a dissatisfaction with the historic person of Jesus and the Jewish limitation of his teaching. To those problems, in due course, the gospel could provide an authoritative response.

The Third Letter is written to Gaius, one of the Elder's supporters in the congregation who has welcomed travelling preachers and is asked to help them on their journey. But he is warned that another member of the congregation, Diotrephes (who is putting himself forward for leadership), rejects the Elder and what he wrote in his letter (i.e., 2 John), and will not welcome the travelling preachers. Very soon the Elder hopes to visit Gaius but meanwhile commends the reliability of Demetrius.

This suggests that the problems indicated in the Second Letter are still present in the congregation and are likely to disrupt it.

1 JOHN

In reading this 'letter' you must remember that the community has now split, according to chapter 2. Some former members have gone out into the world (which means pagan society) – perhaps because they found the community too self-absorbed and thought the world worth saving. At every point the reader should bear in mind that opposing views are being denied. The breakaway group are dissatisfied with the traditional Jewish way of obeying God's laws, but regard themselves as sinless because they have a spiritual anointing (*chrisma*) by which they directly honour God and deny that Jesus is the Christ, that is, *the* Anointed One. The writer of 1 John invents the name 'Antichrists' for them (2:18–19) – they are opponents of Jesus as the person uniquely anointed (*christos*) by God.

1:1–10
The First Letter of John begins with a group statement (indicated by the dominance of the word 'We') which bears testimony to 'eternal

life' – for which the modern idiom might be 'quality life'. It is to be experienced in community and shared with both Father and Son. It provides enlightenment and (not sinlessness but) cleansing from sin by Jesus. This statement is formulated against those who have broken away from the community to experience the darkness of the world, who worship the Father but not the Son, and assert their own sinlessness.

2:1 – 5:12

At this point a father figure takes over, frequently addressing his readers as 'my children' or 'my dear friends' (where the Greek says simply 'my dears'). Each Church is a family gathering of God's children (3:1–3), and the writer calls them 'my children' because he is responsible for them. He knows that they have been disturbed by the breakaway (which seems to have prospered: 'the world listens to them', 4:5) and thrown into doubt by the arguments of the breakaway group. So he takes half a dozen or so fundamental convictions and talks about them, turning them this way and that, exploring a variety of connections, appealing to his readers' self-awareness (2:27). It is not possible to find here a standard presentation, beginning with A, moving on to B and then C, and ending with D. It is more an instructional meditation than an argument. The best I can do is to draw attention to the main convictions.

The writer is constantly aware of the alluring nature and tempting voices of the *world* (i.e., pagan society), though, in the power of the evil one, it is hostile to God and to Christians. But it is passing away, for God has sent his Son into the world to be its saviour and to make atonement for its sins. In the world Christians are as he is, and by their faith in Jesus as Son of God they overcome the world.

It may help if I add to these summaries the passages where the words are mentioned. This will also show how these words dominate the letter, in Greek if not always in English translation.

World   2:2, 15–17; 3:1, 13, 17; 4:1, 3–5, 9, 14, 17; 5:4–5, 19
The opposite of pagan society is life, called *eternal life* because (unlike the world) it is not in decline. God sent his only Son into the world that we might have life through him. Such life must indeed be thought about – but, more than that, it has been displayed, made visible and testified to. It has two essential components: awareness and activity.

Life   1:1–2; 2:25; 3:14–15; 5:11–13, 16, 20
Being aware of life is like passing from darkness to light (2:8–11), or passing from ignorance to *knowledge*. We know we are God's family, but the whole world lies in the power of the evil one. We know that the Son of God has come and given us understanding to know the true God (though the world does not) and we know that this is the last hour of pagan society. We know that everyone who does what is right belongs to God's family. We know God by keeping his *commandments*, namely by practising *love*. We know that we have crossed over from death to life because we *love* our fellow Christians. Anyone who hates his or her fellow walks in the dark and has no idea where he or she is going. But we know that when Christ appears we shall be like him, because we shall see him as he is.

Knowledge   2:3–5, 11, 13, 14, 18, 20, 21, 29; 3:1, 2, 5, 6, 14–16, 19, 20, 24; 4:2, 6–8, 13, 16; 5:13, 15, 18–20

Commandments   2:3, 4, 7, 8; 3:22–24; 4:21; 5:2, 3

Love   2:5, 7, 10, 15; 3:1, 2, 10, 11, 14, 16–18, 21, 23; 4:1, 7–12, 16–21; 5:1–3

But a sinner does not know God and no child of God commits *sin*. Christ appeared in order to take away sin, to plead acceptably for us with God, to be an atonement for all sins (i.e., to do what is necessary to put right what has gone wrong). To deny the Son (as some do) is to be without the Father; to acknowledge the Son is to have the Father too. We need the Son as an example of how to live, of purity, and of self-sacrificing love. He both gives the commandment of love and himself displays it. And *Jesus Christ* is the person who came in the flesh, to whom there are three witnesses: the *Spirit* (who raised him from the dead), the water (of his baptism), and the blood (of his crucifixion).

Sin   1:7–10; 2:1, 2, 12; 3:4–6, 8, 9; 4:10; 5:16–18

Jesus Christ   1:3, 7; 2:1, 2, 8, 22–24; 3:2, 5, 7, 8, 16, 23; 4:2, 3, 9, 10, 14, 15; 5:1, 5, 6–13, 18, 20

Spirit   3:24; 4:1–3, 6, 13; 5:6, 8

5:13–21

Once more eternal life and the world are contrasted, with assurances and warnings – and one pastoral instruction. Of course 'no child of God commits sin', just as no qualified teacher gives an ill-prepared lesson. But anybody can stray, and there has to be a way back to the right path – unless someone knowingly and with determination rejects the Son of God and exploits the power of the evil one. Then the destination is death, not life.

JOHN

The Fourth Gospel is obviously a gospel, but in many ways remarkably unlike the other three. If you have read and considered 2 John and 1 John, you will begin to understand why. Some members had left the community because they were drawn to pagan Greek society and were impatient of interminable Jewish commandments, and because they saw little reason to revere a crucified Jewish holy man when they could directly worship the Father by means of their own anointing with the Spirit. In response the writer of 1 John cannot approve pagan society but he reduces the commandments to 'love one another' (as the gospel does). He gives good reasons why our fellowship is with the Father *and* the Son (a theme powerfully developed in the gospel), and he makes cautious acknowledgement of the Holy Spirit (explicitly treated at length in the Fourth Gospel – in contrast to the other three). The epistle is thus responding to the movement of an originally Jewish gospel into Greek society and then transforming itself into a Greek gospel.

The Fourth Gospel goes much further in reinterpreting the tradition so that it becomes available in Greek society: not only available but also creative. Thus Jesus is no longer the Jewish teacher who provokes thought and response by parables, but the Greek instructor awakening the truth by means of discourses. The Kingdom of God or of Heaven, which dominates teaching in the first three gospels, appears twice at the beginning of John and then disappears. It is replaced by eternal life – that is, life with God in the world above – of which Jesus is the unique guarantor since he is the Son of God and therefore his chief agent. In the Fourth Gospel there is extensive teaching (not tentative as in 1 John or sporadic as in the other gospels) about the Spirit of truth. In this gospel, truth is a dominant concern, built on the conviction that 'truth will set you free' (8:32). For the Jewish leaders (especially those who had to rebuild Judaism after the disasters of 70

CE), to whom the Johannine Jesus shows great hostility, truth was a fence protecting their communal life. For the Johannine Jesus the spirit of truth was an opening into all truth (16:13). But the fourth gospel does not ignore or seek to destroy Jewish tradition – indeed it is (in a Greek idiom) the most subtly Jewish of all New Testament writings – but to make it available to the world in the new epoch inaugurated by the death and resurrection of Jesus.

Basically the fourth gospel tells the same story as the other gospels. Its central character is Jesus of Nazareth, son of Joseph and his mother who are known in the village (1:45; 6:42; 18:5, 7), as are his brothers (2:12; 7:3–10). There is nothing about a virgin birth and the Jerusalem crowd suppose that he was not born in Bethlehem (7:42). He was preceded by John the Baptist, and he recruited and was accompanied by disciples (in all but two chapters). The scene was Galilee, Jerusalem and Samaria, and more than once he was in Jerusalem for the festivals (not first Galilee, then finally, in Jerusalem, as in Mark). He was much in conflict with 'the Jews' which often means the priestly Temple authorities and the lay Pharisees. According to John the first public activity of Jesus was to stage a temple protest – which Mark puts at the end of the story – not so much saying 'That was when it really happened' but 'This is what it was all about'. As for Pharisees, they became the dominant leaders in remaking Jewish life after its ruin in 70 CE. Much that is familiar to us from the first three gospels is not needed by John. There are no unclean spirits, no exorcisms of demon-possessed persons, no tax-collectors and sinners. Jesus is not baptised by John, nor is he subjected in the wilderness to temptations by Satan – but there is something diabolic in some Jewish responses to his teaching, and something Satanic in the actions of a close disciple. There is no episode of transfiguration, but the whole gospel is con-cerned with the lifting up of the Son of Man. At the Last Supper (which is certainly not a Passover meal) there is no explanation of bread and wine – but that had already been given in the synagogue at Capernaum (chapter 6). There is no agony in Gethsemane; but at the Passover, in the presence of Gentiles, Jesus is in turmoil – should he say 'Father, save me from this hour' (12:27)? Then (ch. 17) he says, 'Father, the hour has come', and delivers a confident and majestic report on what he has achieved. There is no trial before the Sanhedrin, and the trial before Pilate is a powerful dramatic presentation which displays fundamental questions about the people of God, secular religion and the government of society.

Two other features emphasised in this gospel are 'signs' and 'I am' sayings.

All the gospels describe what are usually called 'miracles', which means something that we marvel at – and that, of course, depends on our previous state of knowledge. But in the fourth gospel marvels are poorly regarded (4:48) unless they are also *signs*, that is, indications of what lies behind them and what they offer for the future. What lies behind them is the relation of the Son to the Father. What they offer for the future is renewal for the Jewish people. There are seven.

- From repentance to rejoicing in the marriage between God and his people (ch. 2).
- The recovery of life for people at death's door (ch. 4).
- Mobility for a whole generation crippled and hopeless (ch. 5).
- Plentiful nourishment for an eager people deprived of sound instruction (ch. 6).
- Reassurance for people all at sea in the darkness (ch. 6).
- Enlightenment for the needy people who are blind to the truth (ch. 9).
- The conviction that Judaism must be allowed to die before it can be raised to new life (ch. 11) – this final sign corresponding to what Jesus said at 2:19, 'Destroy this temple and in three days I will raise it up again.'

In the other gospels Jesus is notoriously reticent about his identity, but in this gospel he promotes himself openly, sometimes to the Jews in general, sometimes to disciples. There are seven 'I am' sayings when he presents himself as the bread of life (6:35–51), the light of the world (8:12), the door of the sheepfold (10:7), the good shepherd (10:11–14), the resurrection and the life (11:25), the way, the truth and the life (14:6), and the true vine (15:1–5). Similar 'I am' sayings were familiar in popular Greek religion of the time, when the deity disclosed his presence and effect. Jewish readers would pick up echoes from 'I am that I am' in Exodus 3:14, and 'I am the Lord; the Lord is my name' in Isaiah 42:8. John has used this familiar idiom so that Jesus can indicate what to expect from God when we believe his Son – namely nourishment, illumination, protection, recovery from disaster, direction and community.

John was not inventing but translating the Jesus story – which he may have known from reading Mark. Some of his information may derive from independent historical memories, but he was interested not in writing or revising history but in persuading his readers to follow him in thinking out the consequences of faith in Jesus. So we can begin with the Word in 1:1 – the intelligible intention.

1:1–18
The intention of this Prologue is to display the problem for which the gospel is the solution. How can the world (meaning human social existence) possibly reject the divine Wisdom by which it was brought into being? The Prologue outlines the relation between the unseen divine Being and human existence, perhaps referring to the divine Wisdom, perhaps to the human Agent of that Wisdom. It is qualified by referring to the historic prophetic tradition represented by John and completed by testimony from the Christian community to the benefits they received from the divine Sonship.

Understanding the Prologue is indeed the necessary guide to understanding the gospel, but it is also true that the Prologue will be better understood when you have read the whole gospel. Indeed a preliminary understanding of any part of the gospel will be improved when you have tried to respond to the gospel as a whole.

From 1:19 to the end of chapter 12, the gospel represents Jesus responding to 'the world' which in general is insensitive to him – though some recognition became possible, as the next few chapters demonstrate.

1:19 – 4:54
This is an outline of the ministry, located in Judaea, Samaria and Galilee. We are introduced to John the Baptist and his disciples, and to the puzzling success of his baptising ministry. We meet priests, levites and Pharisees, as well as a member of the Jewish Council. From beyond Judaea there are Galileans and Samaritans. We are present at the first of several Jewish festivals, and we observe a surprising protest in the Jerusalem Temple. Recognition for Jesus comes in the form of various names: God's Chosen One, Lamb of God, Rabbi which means Teacher (and of course a teacher has students, or disciples), Messiah (which Jesus acknowledges as true only to a Samaritan woman), Son of God, King of Israel, and a prophet. His only self-reference is Son of Man (which you will begin to understand if you think of Son of God as the true representative of divinity, and Son of Man as the true representative of humanity). There is a thought-provoking balance between earthly and heavenly things, between water and Spirit, between elevation and crucifixion, between light and darkness, between the world insensitive to God yet loved

by him. The appropriate scriptures are indicated, namely the writings of Moses and Isaiah; and the first two signs are displayed (the only 'numbered' signs in the gospel – presumably because they indicate the intention of all the other five). The first sign is given at a family wedding where the water of repentance is turned into the abundant wine of rejoicing – so suggesting what could be done for the whole family of Israel. The second sign is given to an administrative officer whose son was brought back from the point of death – so suggesting what could be done, and needs to be done, for the next generation of Israel.

Chapters 5–12
Jesus and his own Jewish people – put like that to remind us that the hostility, frequently mentioned in this gospel, was part of an inter-Jewish dispute. An excursion into bitterness (ch. 8) may reflect bad relations between a Christian group and Pharisaic teachers trying to rebuild Jewish life after the catastrophe of 70 CE. But according to John, the Jews who heard Jesus were not always hostile (e.g. 8:30, 'many put their faith in him', and 12:9–11) and were sometimes divided in their response (10:19–21; 11:45–46). Most frequently, when John refers to the hostility of the Jews (chs 5–8 and 11) he means the community leaders and (in the passion narrative) the high priests and temple authorities.

This section (with five 'I am' sayings) begins in Jerusalem, goes to Galilee, and then suggests an apparently reluctant transfer to the south. Jewish festivals are mentioned at 5:1; 6:4; 7:2, 8, 10, 11, 14, 37; 10:22; 11:55; 12:1, 12, 20. All who heard the Gospel would know that the Temple had been destroyed and that the sacrifices had not been offered for thirty years.

There is one textual oddity. The story of the woman caught in adultery (7:53 – 8:11) was no original part of this gospel but was a remembered episode, attached for safe-keeping to various points in John and Luke in a variety of ancient manuscripts. The NRSV prints it in its traditional position, but the REB unfortunately prints it separately at the end of the gospel. But this story may have been the first written commentary on this part of the gospel where Jesus speaks with harshness to Jews who had believed in him. In the story Jesus does not condemn an unfaithful woman to death, nor (it may be implied) despite his severity does he so condemn unfaithful Jewish disciples.

Chapter 5

On a festival occasion in Jerusalem, Jesus sees a great number of sick people, hopeless, no longer expecting to be healed except by some odd chance. One is a man crippled for thirty-eight years, and Jesus restores him to mobility – which is obviously a 'sign' to all Israel. When the sign is resisted because on sabbath no work may be done, Jesus insists that God never ceases work – nor does he himself. How then is Jesus related to his Father – on the evidence of John the Baptist, the work God has given to him to do, and the testimony of the scriptures?

Chapter 6

Near Passover time, in heathen territory across the sea from Galilee, 5,000 are fed and the dangers of the sea are overcome. This 'sign' points to the expected prophet, and in the Capernaum synagogue Jesus explains that 'bread' is a symbol of instruction by which people can live. The first 'I am' saying identifies the teacher with his teaching, and with his self-giving. But many of his disciples then refused to follow him, and one was actively hostile.

Chapter 7–8

Near the time of the festival of Tabernacles, Jesus engages in divisive controversy: first with his own brothers in Galilee (7:1–9), then with the festival crowd in Jerusalem, so provoking the chief priests and Pharisees (7:10–52). After 'I am the light of the world' he continues provocatively, and finally treats 'the Jews who had believed him' with extreme severity. As Abraham was the founding father of Israel, so he himself is the predetermined founding father of the new people of God (8:12–59).

Chapter 9

But the blame really lies with the Pharisees (of John's day, not of an earlier time). Ordinary Jews were born blind: by the demands of Pharisaic religion they were not allowed to see the eye-opening, healing power of God. The Pharisees obstinately assert that sight cannot have been repaired because it was done on the sabbath, by a sinful man, of doubtful origins, and whose followers should be banned from the synagogue (that threat appears again at 12:42 and 16:2). The story ends with a fragment of hope for the Pharisees (who were trying to rebuild Jewish life after the disaster of 70 CE) when some of them say 'do you mean that we are blind?' as they come to terms with the sixth sign.

Chapter 10
Opposition to the motives of the Pharisees and their fencing of the synagogue is expressed by the image of the good shepherd (in contrast to the wicked shepherds of Ezekiel 34) who admits those who recognise him to the community, lays down his life for them, and takes up a new life of recognition and enlightenment. At the festival of the Dedication (of the Temple) this again provokes the question, 'Are you the Messiah?' – to which Jesus in effect replies, 'If you belong to my flock of sheep you will know', as many did.

11:1–54
Since death and resurrection has been mentioned in the shepherd imagery, it is now displayed in the story of Lazarus – where it is as much about spiritual death as about physical mortality. The description of the dead man in verse 44, 'his hands and feet bound with linen bandages, his face wrapped in a cloth', could be an image of any Jew bound by Pharisaic rules (as John regarded them); and Jesus' command 'Loose him; let him go' could be the necessary response. When in verse 24 Martha expresses a Pharisaic conviction about 'the resurrection on the last day', Jesus says, 'I am the resurrection and the life. Whosoever has faith in me shall live, even though he dies; and no one who lives and has faith in me shall ever die.'

This is rightly seen as a challenge to the Jewish authorities who convene a meeting (not 'of the Council' which is not mentioned in this gospel) which accepts the cynical but politically astute and theologically correct advice of the high priest.

11:55 – 12:50
The period before *this* Passover is filled with confused emotions and contradictory responses. The authorities want to stop Jesus but admit that they are getting nowhere. The festival pilgrims want to see both Jesus and the revived Lazarus and they excitedly welcome Jesus on his triumphal entry (though the king symbolism provided the charge on which he was condemned), but they are irritated by his self-reference as Son of Man rather than Messiah. His disciples vary between extravagant veneration and self-interested disapproval. When Gentile worshippers surprisingly want to see Jesus, to him this indicates the necessity of his death, and he himself is thrown into

distress. It has to be said that the many signs Jesus performed did not produce faith in him – or at least only timid and frightened faith. So Jesus, as it were, stands aside for people to hear the Father who sent him.

Chapters 13–17
Jesus and the disciples: a compilation written to instruct and warn later Johannine Christians. The section 13:1–35 begins with a communal meal (*before* the Passover), surprisingly interrupted by the foot-washing. Its main theme is loyalty and betrayal. Betrayal is not forgivable but demands the glorifying (i.e., crucifixion) of the Son of Man; and Judas, moved by unappeasable resentment, goes out into the night.

Lesser failings of faithful disciples, such as Peter with his unreflective vigour, can be dealt with if they take to heart the foot-washing and keep the commandment to love one another as Jesus has loved them – though we are now introduced to 'the disciple whom Jesus loved' who is a model of perceptive restraint. (He appears again at 19:26–27; 20:2–9; and 21:7, 20.)

13:36 – 14:31
This both expresses perplexity about the intended departure of Jesus to prepare a place for his disciples and also discloses that involvement with Jesus *is* the way to God. He promises that if they obey his instruction to love one another the Father will give them another sponsor (rather than 'advocate'), the Spirit of truth who will always be with them. This sponsor does not replace Jesus (14:6) but will teach them everything they need to know about the teaching of Jesus. As it is, he gives them peace as his parting gift, and prepares to depart – and we would expect to move at once to chapter 18. But the story-telling is interrupted to provide instruction that will be needed when the earthly story of Jesus is completed.

15:1–17
This deals with love within the community, represented by the vine-imagery of the final 'I am' saying.

15:18–25
The community is warned that the existing social system will be hostile.

15:26 – 16:15
This section promises the help of the advocate or sponsor.

16:16–33
These verses repeat and emphasise the previous teaching about grief and joy.

Chapter 17
The Son reports to the Father and, as it were, provides the charter for the community's existence. Nothing here is said about the death of Jesus or about the Spirit of truth. Instead the prayer is concerned with knowledge and disclosure of the divine name – thus responding to the quest of the Greek world.

Chapters 18–20
These chapters present John's account of the crucifixion and resurrection, in many ways remarkably different from accounts in the other gospels. Chapters 18–19 describe the arrest, Peter's denials, interrogation by the governor and verdict, crucifixion and burial. When this gospel was written, the Jewish authorities had ceased to exist, and all Christians had to face the Roman authorities. In John's account, Jesus is in control throughout and deals with Pilate as man to man. The whole story is told with tragic irony: at point after point what results is the opposite of what was intended by the temple authorities, the Roman governor, the soldiers, even Joseph of Arimathaea. At the end, only Jesus achieves exactly what he intended in caring for his mother and giving up his spirit – but even that was reversed when he rose from the dead and conferred the Holy Spirit (20:22).

Chapter 20 is an enigmatic account of discoveries at the tomb. Two male disciples find only linen wrappings: the disciple whom Jesus loved (who appeared first at the Last Supper and was near the cross (13:23; 19:26–27)) was more perceptive and believing than Peter. But the discovery was first made by a woman follower, Mary of Magdala; and Jesus himself explained to her that he was ascending to the God and Father. Was he, then, the ascended Lord when he conferred the Holy Spirit (much mentioned in the gospel) and the right to forgive and retain sins (not elsewhere mentioned in the gospel – though see Matthew 16:19 and 18:18)? The ascension and gift of the Spirit (which Luke defers till Acts 1 – 2) does not in any way cancel the marks of crucifixion on which life through faith becomes possible.

Chapter 21

This chapter is a resurrection supplement, displaying concerns of the
later community. There is a third appearance of the risen Jesus, a
solemn restoration of Simon Peter and an indication of his martyrdom,
a revised expectation of the beloved disciple and an affirmation of
his written testimony, and a conventional ending. Verses 20–24 refer
to the disciple whom Jesus loved, who was present at the Last Supper
(13:23–25). It was thought that he would live though Peter would
die – but that expectation is firmly corrected, and 'It is this same
disciple who vouches for what has been written here. He it is who
wrote it, and we know that his testimony is true.' 'We' implies the
body of believers who saw the glory (1:14) and who now guarantee
the validity of this new kind of gospel. What did the beloved disciple
assert and write? *Either* what Jesus said about him, *or* the miracle of
the great catch of fish in this supplementary chapter. Perhaps even
more: whatever relies on this disciple's evidence once he appears in
the gospel, probably including the eyewitness of the flow of blood
and water in 19:35. Since he was at the Last Supper he was one of
the Twelve, and according to very ancient tradition he may indeed
have been John Zebedee. But his evidence is a small contribution to
the gospel. The primary author (whoever he was) rethought Mark's
gospel of the Galilean prophet of the last days, and presented Jesus
(in language that devout Greeks could follow) as the revealer of our
pathway to the eternal world.

9 Later Writings

JAMES

This is obviously not really a letter but an apparently unsystematic notebook, dealing with moral and pastoral questions in a Jewish manner. It assumes that Christianity is dispersed (like Judaism) throughout the Roman world, and its author is James who frequently addresses his readers as 'my brothers' (the REB says 'friends', the NRSV has 'brothers and sisters') or 'my beloved' – except when he intends rebuke, and then it is 'adulterers' and 'sinners'. This looks like a useful handbook for dealing with Christian communities, modelled on the teaching in Matthew's gospel, when they run into trouble of various kinds. There are five people called James in the New Testament, but only James the brother of Jesus is sufficiently well known to head this writing. He saw the risen Christ (1 Cor. 15:7), became prominent in the Jerusalem Church (Acts 15:13; 21:18; Gal. 1:19; 2:9, 12 – Paul found him tiresome for sending messengers to Antioch who persuaded Peter no longer to share meals with Gentile Christians), and, according to the Jewish historian Josephus, was martyred in 62 CE. By that time the Christians were scarcely 'dispersed throughout the world'.

James 'a servant of God and the Lord Jesus Christ' refers in 2:1 (the Greek is odd) to faith 'in our Lord Jesus Christ who reigns in glory'. Otherwise there is no mention of his life, death and resurrection. When an example is needed of suffering and patience, James turns to the prophets and Job (5:10–11), but there are echoes of the Matthean tradition of the teaching of Jesus: for example, do not use oaths (which call on God as witness) but simply plain 'Yes' or 'No' (5:12, as in Matt. 5:34–37). 'James' is undoubtedly a Christian writing, no doubt carrying on the tradition of Jesus' brother who became a kind of Caliph for the Jewish Christians. It was put into writing – very good

Greek – after his death, when Jewish Christian communities had fallen into a depressing state. To our minds there is no orderly sequence of ideas, but an alert reader will pick up frequent cross references that would have seemed properly persuasive to its earliest hearers.

1:2–4
All sorts of trials.

1:5–8
Wisdom for dealing with the trials.

1:9–11
Poor and wealthy church members.

1:12–15
Trials that are self-generated.

1:16–18
Good benefits come from the Father who brought us to birth by the *word* of truth.

1:19–21
Be quick to hear, slow to speak, accept the implanted *word*.

1:22–25
Be doers of the *word*, not only hearers. If any are hearers of the word and not performers, they are like people regarding the face they were born with in a mirror: they regard themselves and then go away and [absurdly] forget what they were like. But those who make the effort of looking into the perfect *law* of liberty – and stay with it, becoming not forgetful hearers but active performers – such will be happy in their activity.

1:26–27
Pure and faultless religion is controlling your tongue, caring for orphans and widows in trouble (picking up 'trials', 1:2–4), and keeping yourself untarnished by the cosmos, that is, the prevailing habits of society.

2:1–7
This takes up the poor/wealthy theme of 1:9–11.

2:8–13
These verses take up the 'word' theme of 1:8–23 and especially 'law' of 1:25. The sovereign law, according to scripture, is 'love your neighbour as yourself'. Partiality breaks that law, and to break one law is to break all law. The perfect law that makes us free (1:25) is so called because mercy triumphs over judgement.

2:14–26
Faith and action.

3:1–12
Picks up 1:19, 26 on the danger of the tongue.

3:13–18
Picks up 1:5–8 on wisdom.

4:1–10
This section picks up the cosmos theme of 1:27; 2:5; 3:6. Fighting and quarrels are the self-generated trials of 1:12–15. In verse 5 it is not possible to identify the supposed 'scripture' (look perhaps at Wisdom 2:24; 6:23) or to know how to translate the Greek (the REB and NRSV are totally opposed).

4:11–12
Picks up the law theme of 2:8–12.

4:13–17
Picks up the 'wealthy' of 1:9–11 in opposition to self-confident entrepreneurs.

5:1–6
Denounces the oppressive and uncaring wealthy, in an age near its close.

5:7–11
Picks up 1:2–4 and advises patience until the Lord comes.

5:12–14

Oaths (which are a means of dragging God into the life of the community) are forbidden. Instead prayer, anointing, confession and pastoral concern are commended.

At that point the instruction suddenly stops.

In the most attractive tradition of Jewish religion this writer sets out the social consequences of being Christian. To have faith is to devote oneself to a demanding set of initiatives and responses. 'Anyone who knows the right thing to do and does not do it is a sinner' (4:17). If only it were so simple! James seems unaware of the wrong we may do when confidently doing what seems right – as Paul discovered. If 'faith divorced from action is dead' (as James says, 2:26), then reliance on ourselves, rather than on the saving goodness of God, can be ruinous.

PASTORAL EPISTLES

Paul's main letters are addressed to Christian communities. Even the very personal letter to Philemon is addressed to the Church that meets in his house. But the letters to Timothy and Titus are addressed to *individual* church leaders who are to carry out Paul's instructions in Ephesus and Crete and, in 2 Timothy and Titus, are to give Paul's greetings to the local Churches. The situation they presume cannot be found in the information we have (in Acts and Paul's church letters) about Paul's life *before* his arrest. So they presume that he was released (as suggested in 2 Timothy 4:16) and resumed travelling – but in the eastern Mediterranean, not in the West as he had intended when mentioning Spain in Romans 15:24.

TITUS

From Galatians 2:1 and 3 we know that Titus was an uncircumcised Gentile who accompanied Paul and Barnabas when they went from Antioch to consult the Christian leaders in Jerusalem (the apostolic consultation described in Acts 15). He became very important as Paul's agent in dealing with the vexing problems of the Corinthian Church (2 Cor. 2:13; 7:6, 13–15; 8:6, 16; 12:18): 'Titus is my partner and my fellow-worker in dealing with you' (2 Cor. 8:23). It is therefore not surprising that Titus should have been left behind in Crete to deal with outstanding matters and in particular to appoint elders in accordance with the principles Paul had laid down (Tit. 1:5). But we have no other information that Paul evangelised Crete, and he never mentions 'elders' in his church letters. ('Elders' is a favourite Lukan word, which he associates with Paul in Acts 14:23.) That oddity might be overlooked, but a close view of the letter produces some discomfort.

1:1–4
A surprisingly complex and heavy-handed greeting in a personal letter to a long-time fellow worker

1:5
Why Titus was left in Crete.

1:6
Qualifications of elders.

1:7–9
Qualifications of a bishop (overseer) as God's steward.

1:10–16
Intemperate remarks about Jewish converts, Cretans and unbelievers.

2:1
Titus is to provide wholesome instruction (as if he didn't know!).

2:2–10
Qualities of good church members, disclosing that the reputation of the Gospel depends on the submissiveness of women and slaves. Titus (surely no longer a young man) is to set young men a good example.

2:11–14
Part of a creed.

2:15
Titus' authority.

3:1–2
Christians to be submissive, timid and gentle.

3:3
A stock confession of past immorality, unsuitable to Paul (Phil. 3:6).

3:4–8
Part of another creed, marked as 'a reliable saying'.

3:9–11
Christians should devote themselves to good works and not become involved in controversial questions.

3:12–15
Personal comments and greetings – which sound like the standard ending of a Pauline letter.

Those random jottings seem to indicate a group of converts who formerly belonged to the immoral pagan world which they now partly despise, partly fear. Titus has authority (a) to provide wholesome instruction, partly in credal form; and (b) to approve church leaders by well-known standards, to lay down rules of conduct: being submissive to the authorities, devoted to good works, and not engaged in controversy – claiming always the approval of Paul.

TIMOTHY

After the Jerusalem consultation already mentioned, Paul revisited Churches in Syria and Cilicia. At Lystra (Acts 16:1–3) he added to his group of assistants a Christian called Timothy, son of a Jewish Christian mother (he was therefore a Jew) and a Gentile father. When Timothy had been circumcised (out of consideration for local Jewish residents) he accompanied Paul as he crossed over to Macedonia, where he is named as one of Paul's representatives (Acts 17:14–15; 18:5; 19:22; 20:4). This is confirmed by remarks in 1 Thessalonians 3:2, 6 (the earliest letter) and Philippians 2:19 (the latest letter). Even more significantly, Timothy helps Paul in his awkward relations with Corinth: 'I have sent Timothy, who is a dear son to me and a trustworthy Christian' (1 Cor. 16:10–11). And finally, Timothy is a joint author with Paul in 1 and 2 Thessalonians, 2 Corinthians, Philippians, Colossians and Philemon. Timothy was therefore a long-term assistant and intimate of Paul.

That relation shows better in the second letter than in the first.

2 TIMOTHY

1:1–2
A rather formal greeting.

1:3–5
A thanksgiving such as is normally found at the beginning of a Pauline letter. This is a long, complex, poorly organised sentence in un-Pauline language.

1:6–14
A miscellany of instructions – many of which seem unnecessary for Timothy: did he need to be reminded to stir up the flame, or to be told that Paul had been appointed herald, apostle and teacher?

1:15–18
Credible personal news.

2:1–13
A collection of personal instructions. But did Timothy need to be urged to take his share of hardship, to remember the theme of Paul's Gospel (with two credal fragments)?

2:14–26
A jumble of instructions, moralising reflections, and commonplace illustrations. How could Timothy be told to 'turn from the wayward passions of youth' when (by the standards of his time) he was at least a middle-aged man?

3:1–5
A denunciation of the morals of the final age (presumably now beginning) with a conventional list of vices – implying that the writer intends to do nothing except denounce them.

3:6–9
The insidious danger of delusive teachers (nothing more than fools) who entrance foolish women (reflecting the common Hellenistic prejudice against women). Jannes and Jambres (Egyptian magicians who opposed Moses) are from Jewish legends.

3:10–13

A stock-list of virtues, including fortitude in persecution at Antioch, Iconium and Lystra, that is, in the early days of Acts 13:50 and 14:5–6, 19. Since then there had been much more suffering as Paul relates in 2 Corinthians 11:23–27 – of which letter Timothy was a joint author.

3:14–17

Timothy is encouraged to stand by the truths he had learned and to make suitable use of the Jewish scriptures (which he had known from early childhood) for doctrine and morals.

4:1–5

The commissioning of a new gospel preacher.

4:6–8

A martyr's farewell – that is blown away by what follows.

4:9–21

The sort of personal news that is expected at the end of a Pauline letter. The writer, though in a depressed mood, expects Timothy to join him before long and believes that the Lord will rescue him from all harm.

1 TIMOTHY

1:1–2

A formal greeting in un-Pauline language.

1:3–7

Without the standard Pauline thanksgiving, the writer says that Timothy was left behind in Ephesus to thwart certain people and their wrong teaching which has something to do with the Law and not much with genuine faith. This is obscurely expressed.

1:8–11

Some entirely un-Pauline comments on the Law.

1:12–17

An account of Paul's conversion – did Timothy need to be told that? If Paul sinned in ignorance could he stand first among sinners?

1:18–20
The writer begins a charge to Timothy, but is waylaid by the memory of two lapsed Christians.

2:1–7
This concerns community prayers, particularly for the authorities, so that the community, practising its religion, can be tranquil. Does Timothy need to be vehemently assured that Paul was appointed apostle to the Gentiles?

2:8–15
Rules about community behaviour, especially about the dress and submission of women. In Greek the meaning of verse 15 is very obscure.

3:1–13
Conventional qualities of church leaders.

3:14–15
The reason for writing: in case Paul is delayed in returning to Ephesus, he tells Timothy what is proper conduct in God's household. But surely Timothy and Ephesus (where Paul had spent much time) already knew.

3:16
Part of a creed.

4:1–5
Anxiety about moving into a period of immorality and asceticism is soothed by remembering the goodness of the creation.

4:6–10
A miscellany of well-intended remarks, one of them needlessly offensive to older women.

4:11–16
More from the same stock – with the astonishing remark 'Let no one undervalue you because you are young'. Admirable in general, but incredible of Timothy.

5:1–2
How a young man should treat community members.

5:3–16
Elaborate though unsystematic proposals for dealing with widows who when young may become 'idle, gossips and busybodies' – but so, of course, may men.

5:17–22
On dealing with elders.

5:23–25
Odds and ends.

6:1–2
On slaves.

6:3–5
Conventional disapproval of rival teachers.

6:6–10
The real benefits of religion, as against the love of riches.

6:11–16
Perhaps an ordination liturgy.

6:17–19
A caution to the wealthy.

6:20–21
An appeal to Timothy which, surely, he scarcely needed. But it rounds off the letter.

According to 2 Timothy 1:5, Timothy was a third-generation Christian and we know that he was an experienced colleague of Paul. Much that is written in 1 and 2 Timothy would have been inappropriate, at this stage, to the original Timothy. So the letters present a dramatic rather than an actual setting. Moreover, the Greek wording is notably different from the vocabulary of Paul's church letters. So too is the letter pattern. Paul's normal pattern is: introduction, thanksgiving, theological argument, advice about conduct, and farewell greetings.

Here there is no theological argument, but much advice about conduct though fragmentary and poorly arranged. Hence it is difficult to think that Paul was the actual writer of these letters. How then to account for them?

In the background of the letters are place names familiar to readers of Acts: Antioch, Iconium, Lystra, Galatia, Ephesus, Troas, Thessalonica and Corinth. They mark out the area of Paul's missionary preaching – where, however, the Pauline structure is in danger of collapse (e.g. 2 Tim. 1:15). The self-governing Christian communities were responding uncertainly to changing circumstances. So it seemed necessary to pass on to them a varied collection of community instructions (Jewish, Gentile and Christian) for the encouragement of a younger generation of area leaders – of whom Timothy, in his earliest association with Paul, is the model. The 'Timothy' for whom the letters were written was a dispirited young man, expected to suffer hardship for the Gospel (so he is reminded of Paul's plight and hardships). People oppose him and he needs to discipline them. He is perplexed by the demands and activity of women, and by the pride of the wealthy. There is much disputing about words and silly religious chatter. He must keep from speculation and stick to sound teaching and credal statements. If things are going badly wrong, that is to be expected at the end of the age.

If the writer indeed knew Acts, the date of the Pastoral Epistles might be about 100 CE. At that time, it would seem, it had again become necessary to defend Paul's Gospel as a genuine outreach of 'the faith of God's chosen people' (Tit. 1:1–3 – see also Tit. 1:10–11; 3:3, 9; 2 Tim. 1:3, 5, 11; 3:15–17; 4:7; 1 Tim. 1:12–17). But also he and his Gospel were doing badly: he was deserted and unsupported (2 Tim. 1:15; 4:10–18), there were lapsed Christians (1 Tim. 1:20) and rival teachers (1 Tim. 1:7; 2 Tim. 3:6–9; 4:3) with delusive teachings (2 Tim. 2:17–18; 1 Tim. 1:3–4; 4:1–3; 6:3–5, 20–21). And the Christian community was settling down to dwell quietly in pagan society (1 Tim. 2:1–2; 6:17–19).

What are we to make of this for our response today? *First*, there are credal passages that we can wholeheartedly accept (Tit. 2:11–14; 3:4–8; 2 Tim. 2:8, 11–13; 1 Tim. 1:15–17; 3:16; 6:11–16). *Second*, we can compare the troubles of our present Churches with the troubles of a Christian Church not a century old – and take courage. But we must find our own solutions, not try to adopt theirs. *Third*, there are warning indications of what happens when Christians intend to settle down quietly in society as it is.

JUDE

The author of this brief letter to unidentified Christians calls himself 'Jude, servant of Jesus Christ and brother of James'. Presumably that points to Matthew 13:55, 'Is not he the carpenter's son? Is not his mother called Mary, his brothers James, Joseph, Simon, and Judas?' (similarly in Mark 6:3). This letter seems to be another communication from what might be called the Caliphate of James (see above p. 108). It is a tirade – which starts off most alarmingly but ends up more conventionally. Some people have sneaked in (v. 4); they are ungodly, they pervert free grace and become licentious. They are deluded dreamers (v. 8) who defile their bodies, flout authority, insult celestial beings, and pour abuse on whatever they do not understand (v. 10). In some ways they are a bad influence at love-feasts (v. 12). They are grumblers and malcontents, bombastic, given to flattery (v. 16). They cause divisions, are worldly and unspiritual (v. 19).

If this seems an improbable description of a Christian community, it is after all what must be expected in the final age (v. 18) – and it has happened before. When God rescued his people from Egypt he destroyed unbelievers (Num. 14). The sexually disobedient angels of Genesis 6:1–4 were chained in perpetual darkness according to 1 Enoch 6–19 (a writing from the second century BCE). The shameful sexuality of Sodom and Gomorrah (Gen. 19) was punished by eternal fire. The archangel Michael showed respect for a divine being even though he *was* the devil (a Jewish legend – according to early church fathers – recorded in a now lost section of the first-century CE writing, the Assumption of Moses). Warnings can also be found in the fate of Cain (Gen. 4), in the fate of Balaam who enticed Israel into apostasy (Num. 22 – 25), and in the fate of Korah who led a revolt against God (Num. 16). The intruders are the wandering stars and the godless of 1 Enoch 14–15, 18, 21 and 90. From this it would seem that Jude gave a measure of scriptural authority to such writings as 1 Enoch.

What then are the community to do? They are to struggle for the faith (v. 3), to remember the apostolic predictions about the final age (vv. 17–18), to make the most sacred faith the foundation of their lives (v. 20), to pray in the power of the Holy Spirit and to look forward to the mercy of the Lord Jesus Christ that leads to eternal life (v. 21). They are to exercise pity for some doubting souls, save others by snatching them from the flames – though sometimes mixing pity with fear, hating even the clothing defiled by the flesh (whatever that implies).

This very disturbed and disturbing writing ends with the noblest doxology in the New Testament.

2 PETER

This is probably the latest New Testament writing. If the apostolic age ended with the destruction of Jerusalem in 70 CE, and the post-apostolic age with (say) 110, what followed was the age of the early Church – where 2 Peter belongs.

It purports to be written by Simeon Peter as his second letter (3:1) though in the first letter he calls himself simply Peter. 'Simeon' is an archaic form (nearer the Hebrew) and elsewhere is attached to Peter only in Acts 15:14 (see the NRSV) by James when presiding at the apostolic consultation. The writer presents himself as having seen the transfiguration of Jesus (1:16–18 – see the parallel accounts in Mathew 17, Mark 9 and Luke 9), and he now regards his own death as near (1:13–15). Therefore what he produces looks like a farewell message or 'testament' – a kind of writing that was well known in Jewish and Christian circles at this time. But this was an imaginative kind of writing, suggesting what great figures of the past would want to say to people in the present time.

There are strong reasons for concluding that the 'letter' could not have been written by Peter himself:

- Chapter 2 uses and is dependent on the Letter of Jude.
- In 3:3–4 there are people who complain that the promised coming of the Lord has still not happened despite the passage of time.
- Readers of 2 Peter know a collection of Paul's letters which are regarded as 'scripture' (3:15–16) – certainly not in Peter's lifetime. And in any case, the interpretation of scripture has become a problem (1:20).
- The letter has a number of Greek rather than Jewish religious ideas, for example becoming participants of the divine nature (1:4 NRSV).
- The letter is not referred to in any Christian writing before the third century, and even then as disputed. The great biblical scholar Jerome (of the late third century) says that it is 'rejected by the majority because in style it is incomparable with the former letter'.

Whoever may have been the genuine author of the letter and whatever its original purpose, it remains truly part of the New Testament. Its function is not to provide obligatory beliefs but obligatory questions, to which (with the rest of the New Testament before them) modern Christians must find their own answers.

1:1–2
Greeting.

1:3–11
Christian development: method and results.

1:12–15
Peter's testament begins.

1:16–18
Peter's eye-witness authority.

1:19–21
That authority supported by prophetic writings when properly, not privately, understood.

2:1–22
False prophets in the past correspond to false teachers now. They are trounced, denounced, and set up for destruction.

3:1–16
But the false teachers had a damaging objection to apostolic expectations. The first Christian generation had passed away: 'What has happened to the promise of his coming?' To this there are some embarrassed answers. Had not 'Paul, our dear friend and brother' said that 'the world as we know it is passing away' (1 Cor. 7:31)? (i) Well, it once happened with the waters of the flood. It could happen now by fire (perhaps volcanically, with Vesuvius in 79 CE as the preliminary). (ii) By the delay, God's patience is providing an opportunity for repentance and salvation (not easily discoverable in Paul's letters). (iii) Psalm 90:4 says that in God's sight 'a thousand years are as the passing of one day' – so that long delay for us is but brief time for the Lord. (iv) But take no chances; the day of the Lord will come like a thief.

3:17–18
It looks as if the 'dear friends' are Churches founded by Paul's evangelistic energy, perhaps still respectful of his memory and letters

though now troubled by internal disagreements. The parallel (perhaps rival) Petrine group stretch out a helping hand – though mention that it was Peter who saw the transfigured Jesus, and remark that Paul's letters 'contain some obscure passages, which the ignorant and unstable misinterpret to their own ruin'.

These two epistles, the latest additions to the canonical New Testament, are scarcely agreeable reading. Instead of 'devout and dedicated lives' (2 Pet. 3:11) they show inner anxiety and outward insensitivity – the unpleasantness of sectarian religion. They are not a model for present readers but a warning: this is what we Christians look like to unbelieving neighbours and the media – especially if we imply that God was being patient with us while the Holocaust was taking place, or more recent massacres happened in Central Africa, or while long ago we profited from the slave trade . . . and so on. At the end, 2 Peter says 'Do not lose your own safe foothold.' How safe is it?

PSEUDONYMITY

There is another problem that modern readers often find perplexing, namely pseudonymity, that is, writings put out under a fictitious name. If the Letter of Jude is a very late addition to the New Testament, could its author have been Judas, the brother of Jesus and of James? As for 2 Peter, the author cannot be identical with the author of 1 Peter – and, in turn, was he Peter, the companion of Jesus? Thirteen letters bear Paul's name, but was Colossians written, or only approved, by him? Ephesians was most probably not written by him, nor were the Pastoral Epistles. It is, of course, not very important to know who the writers were. Hebrews is a wonderful writing but we do not know its author. We know that Revelation was written by John, but who he was we do not know. Certainly not the author of the fourth gospel, nor of any of the Johannine epistles. The gospels do not name their authors: ancient tradition may be right in naming Mark and Matthew; and Luke was the self-conscious author of two volumes (though without naming himself). In a sense, none of this matters: the Holy Spirit was prompting and guiding each writer, and we respond to the quality of what they wrote.

No embarrassment occurs if the named author is giving his approval to what a colleague or secretary has composed at his request or under his influence. For example, in 1 Peter 5:12 the writer says: 'I write you this brief letter through Silvanus, whom I know to be a trustworthy colleague.' So (it has been suggested), perhaps Silvanus was the ghost writer. Though that is not persuasive, it points in the right direction. It is likely that Colossians and Ephesians were written as developments of Paul's theological teaching; and the Pastoral Epistles were compiled as a necessary adaptation of Paul's missionary strategy. Paul, of course, was not the only prominent figure in early Christianity. In Acts, Peter plays a leading part in the early stages, and James remains an eminent figure. It is credible that letters were written with respect for the memory of James and Peter. Jude is surprising. It suggests that the family of Jesus was trying to keep hold of the tradition initiated and prompted by Jesus, resisting outside interest.

As far as the New Testament epistles are concerned, we shall be acceptably traditional if we refer to:

- epistles of Paul and the Pauline school;
- epistle of a liturgical writer (Hebrews);
- epistles of the Petrine school;
- epistles of the Jesus family tradition;
- epistles of the Johannine School.

10 How Should We Read?

There, then, are the New Testament writings, spread out over a period of fifty-five years from 50 to 105 CE, some before and some after the destruction of Jerusalem in the year 70. These are genuine historic writings. According to Christian conviction, they are able to bring us uniquely into contact with the God who is known in Jesus Christ. But it is *our* contact, not the contact of Paul or James or John. When we read each verse which belongs to the remote past, we must rethink what the author is saying in his day so that it becomes what we say in our day.

It is, of course, true that the imagery used of God in the Bible was appropriate for ancient ways of life; but God is eternal, not antique. (Paul speaks of 'his everlasting power and deity' and of 'the eternal God', Rom. 1:20; 16:26.) Jesus indeed lived and died an ancient Galilean Jew, but 'being raised from the dead, will never die again' (Rom. 6:9). And, 'if the Spirit of him who raised Jesus from the dead dwells in you, then the God who raised Christ Jesus from the dead will also give new life to your mortal bodies through his indwelling Spirit' (Rom. 8:11). New life, not antique life!

If therefore I persuade you to read the various writings of the New Testament in their historical settings, I would then encourage you to rethink what you have read. The model is the New Testament itself. What Paul wrote in 1 Thessalonians was rethought and rewritten in 2 Thessalonians. The rich, varied and complex material in 1 Corinthians was rethought and rewritten in 2 Corinthians. Indeed the first half of 2 Corinthians is movingly rewritten in the second half. The powerful and contentious material of Galatians was expanded in Romans and developed into a comprehensive presentation of the Gospel for Jews and Gentiles and a heartbroken plea for Israel. The enquiring and speculative theology of Colossians is rethought and rounded out in Ephesians. The pastoral instruction of Titus and 2

Timothy is developed with more formality in 1 Timothy. The distressed outcry in Jude is given a more understandable context in 2 Peter, perhaps in response to the 'fiery ordeal' of 1 Peter 4:12.

Mark was a pioneer. What he wrote determined what a gospel should be – even when Matthew and Luke used it, rethought it and rewrote it in different ways. Mark was still the model even when John, prompted by the moral and spiritual problems of 1 John, wrote his gospel in a new Hellenistic style. Even Revelation, in chapters 2 and 3, is a rethinking of what Paul and John's elder were doing when they wrote letters to their Churches; and then it undertakes a comprehensive rethinking of Mark 13 and the Book of Daniel.

What then is our rethinking response to these New Testament writings – a double response of thinking how the author got to where he is and how we rethink his thoughts for our own situation? Allow me to offer some possible examples.

GALATIANS 3:28

There is no longer Jew or Greek, there is no longer slave or free, there is no longer male or female; but you are all one in Christ Jesus. (NRSV, which is closer to Paul than the REB)

What Paul says to the Churches of the Galatian region is revised and expanded in a later letter to another Church in Asia Minor, namely Colossian's (3:11). To 'Greek and Jew' the writer adds 'circumcised and uncircumcised', he omits 'male and female' and substitutes 'barbarian, Scythian' – the latter (living in what we call southern Russia) having a very barbaric reputation.

How *could* Paul bring himself to say that 'there is no longer Jew or Greek'? Brought up in a devout Jewish home, a young enthusiast for Jewish ancestral traditions, he must daily have contrasted himself with the idolatry and immorality of Greek life. To him Abraham was the founding father of his people. It was Abraham who first bore the distinguishing mark of circumcision (Gen. 17:9–14). How could he say (or encourage his associates to say) there is no longer circumcised and uncircumcised? He hints at the reason in Galatians 2:15–17: God wanted a different apostle, a Jew brought up among Gentiles, to be an apostle to the Greeks.

What then does Paul imply in saying 'there is no longer slave or free'? He himself was a free man, and born a Roman citizen (Acts 22:25–29) but he knew that the Empire depended on the work of slaves and the repression of slave dissidence. He could send a slave back to his master though as 'more than a slave, as a brother beloved' (Philemon 16). And he himself (in a very non-Greek way) knew what it was to experience enslavement to God (Rom. 6:22). What had he in mind in saying 'no longer slave or free'? The writer of Colossians adds the social division between Greek and barbarian, between the pride of civilised Greeks and the crude babble of barbarous languages and their repulsive customs – which Paul might have felt. After all he was not only a Roman citizen (and Romans could behave barbarously) but also a notable composer of Hellenistic letters.

And what could he imply by saying 'there are no longer male and female'? From his extensive travels he knew better than many that men had the responsibility for public affairs, from the local council to defending the Empire's frontiers in the army; and that women were required to stay at home and defeat the excessive death rate by producing more children. Within the bounds of what was publicly possible Paul did more for the status and community activity of women than any other person.

What Paul has done is to indicate the conflicts of race, society and human sexuality and say that in Christ Jesus they turn from hostility to co-operation. When people act together in Christ Jesus, the saving power released by death and resurrection is at work: the hostility dies and the co-operation springs into life.

Paul's situation is not ours but, having thought our way into his, we are under obligation to work out our own – if, that is, we wish to be in Christ Jesus. Our situation seems much more complex: not simply Jew and Greek but American lifestyle versus European culture and languages; residual Christianity versus confident Islam; black communities with people born and bred in Britain; the Irish and the British, and the self-awareness of Scotland and Wales in contrast with the English. Our common life is not nominally dependent on slavery and freedom, but we have our desperately poor and our very well-to-do. Male and female, of course, but much marred by aggression and sexual obsession. Perhaps in such times as these we need to rethink Galatians 3:28.

MATTHEW 5:39–41 AND LUKE 6:29–30

What I tell you is this:
Do not resist those who wrong you.

If anyone slaps you on the right cheek, turn and offer him the other also.
If anyone wants to sue you and takes your shirt, let him have your cloak as well.
If someone in authority presses you into service for one mile, go with him two.
(Matthew 5:39–41 REB)

[If anyone hits you on the cheek, offer the other also; if anyone takes your cloak, let him have your shirt as well.
(Luke 6:29 REB)]

These well-known but perplexing words belong to Matthew's Sermon on the Mount. The second half of verse 39 and verse 40 have closely similar sayings in Luke's Sermon on the Plain. To whom were they spoken?

From Matthew 5:1 it is not clear whether Jesus escaped from the crowds or whether he taught them; but 7:28–29 suggests that he taught the crowds, not only disciples. Luke 6:17 refers to 'a large crowd of his disciples' to whom he spoke (Luke 6:20) and 'when he had finished addressing the people, he entered Capernaum' (7:1). Thus both Matthew and Luke imply that this was teaching for disciples, made available to all hearers. But in my judgement, if it was appropriate for everyone to know what Jesus required of his disciples, his requirements were not binding on all his hearers.

It is well known that Jesus went about Galilee, announcing the availability of the sovereign rule of God (Mark 1:14–15). The same story is told in Luke 9:1–6 and more elaborately in Matthew 9:37 – 10:16, ending with a warning about the risk and dangers of their mission: 'I send you out like sheep among wolves; be wary (or, wise) as serpents, innocent as doves.' Later, according to Luke (10:1–16), Jesus 'appointed a further seventy-two and sent them on ahead in pairs to every town and place he himself intended to visit' – again with the warning 'I am sending you like lambs among wolves'.

A slap on the right cheek must (from a right-handed person) be backhanded, and thus specially insulting. How are they to behave when they are met with indignity, rapacity or forced labour? Accept the insult, by offering the other cheek, because you cannot present the sovereign rule of God to someone with whom you are indignant.

As for clothing: Jewish men wore a linen or woollen shirt next to the skin, and an outer cloak which also served as a nightly blanket.

Matthew has in mind the Jewish practice of seizing a garment as a pledge (Exod. 22:26–27); Luke thinks simply of theft. Rather than trying to offer the sovereign rule of God while insisting on your rights, just stand naked!

If the Roman soldiers are compelling civilians to do their bidding and carry their equipment, they should not resist or complain. They cannot present the sovereign rule of God if they are being beaten by the soldiers.

Of course, there was a proper legal remedy for such hardships. The law of 'an eye for an eye, a tooth for a tooth' (Matt. 5:38, quoted from Exod. 21:24; Lev. 24:20; Deut. 19:21) may long ago have implied savage reprisals. But in the time of Jesus it was taken to indicate compensation according to damage. Jesus says, in effect, 'Do not demand compensation for insult, rapacity, and forced labour.' There is no suggestion that turning the other cheek, offering to be naked, going the second mile will embarrass the offenders, or rouse their admiration, or convert them into friends. They are just as likely to become more offensive. Jesus *intends* what he says to be shocking. God's sovereign rule is not to be presented by people who are safe-guarding their own dignity, maintaining their own comfort, or asserting their own freedom. This is a protest against the violence endemic in society.

These words of Jesus were addressed to a small number of enthusiasts in Galilee. They were put into practice by Jesus himself before Jewish and Roman authorities in Jerusalem. For three hundred years they informed a threatened and martyred Church. Then, with the Emperor Constantine, Christianity became the religion of the Empire. Should these words be literally applied or given a modest re-interpretation? That question divided the Church between minority groups and the main establishments. In our own day, when the Churches we know best are in trouble and decline, what are we to make of these sayings?

If we can give meaning to 'the sovereign rule of God' (a substitute for the old-fashioned and misleading 'Kingdom of God'), it will at least imply that the Almighty demands action for those who are poor and suffering, and promises them not only relief but also glory ('Thine is the Kingdom, the power and the glory'). If the Churches do that not only for their adherents but also for society (which is what the New Testament means by 'world' or 'cosmos'), are they careful to safeguard their pride? Do they protest at the reduction of their resources and privileges? Do they decline to get involved in the rough-house of local life? Or do they astutely use their weakness to bring down hostile powers? Paul did: 'I am content with a life of weakness, insult, hardship, persecution, and distress, all for Christ's sake; for when I am weak, then I am strong' (2 Cor. 12:10).

HEBREWS 6:4–6

For when people have once been enlightened when they have tasted the heavenly gift and have shared in the Holy Spirit, when they have experienced the goodness of God's word and the spiritual power of the age to come, and then after all this have fallen away, it is impossible to bring them afresh to repentance; for they are crucifying to their own hurt the Son of God and holding him up to mockery.

(REB. NRSV is a little closer to the Greek, but it abandons the dramatic rhetoric of the passage.)

The writer has interrupted his theological exposition in order to reproach his readers for their failure to make progress in understanding the faith. They are still infants wanting milk instead of adults taking solid food. 'Let us stop discussing the rudiments of Christianity,' he says. 'Instead, let us advance towards maturity.' But why not leave them with their 'simple faith'? Because immature faith, encountering adult problems, is in danger of withering and collapsing. The final state of such people is worse than their former condition, and the writer of Hebrews is alarmed at the dangers: 'We are bound to pay all the more heed to what we have been told, for fear of drifting from our course' (2:1).

He sets out what becoming a Christian has conferred upon them. They have been enlightened. Later he reminds them of the 'early days when newly enlightened, you met the test of great suffering and held firm' (10:32). In a perplexing and hostile world they received illumination. They were not baffled and despairing, for they had some confident understanding of what was going on.

They had tasted *the heavenly gift* – which may mean that they had begun to savour the graciousness, the unutterable kindness of God. Or (as the ancient church fathers said) they had tasted the eucharistic food – indicating that the bodily life of Christ was given for them and to them. They had shared *in the Holy Spirit* by which the instruction of scripture and its promises were made attractively plain (e.g. 9:8).

They had experienced *the goodness of God's word* which created the

world and sustains it (11:3; 1:3) and *the powers of the new phase* of
human experience.

That is an impressive description of being a Christian – cast in the
form not of making demands but of conferring benefits. If now they
fell away, they would not simply be returning to traditional Judaism
or commonplace paganism – not goods on sale or return but perma-
nently damaged goods. They would have experienced the promised
benefits of Christian faith and found them inadequate, or unreliable,
or false, or too challenging. Since the death and exaltation of Christ
is at the heart of Christian faith (certainly as the writer of Hebrews
explains it) such people – these apostates – would be deriding the
crucifixion. As others had done when it took place. But of them it
could be said, 'Father, forgive them for they know not what they do'
(Luke 23:34). But these apostates know what they are doing 'since on
their own they are crucifying again the Son of God (NRSV – or
'crucify to their own hurt the Son of God', REB) and holding him up
to mockery'. It is impossible to bring them afresh to repentance.

To us, repentance implies regret or remorse. In biblical Greek it
means a change of mind, a complete turn-about – which often may
be just what is needed. But if, for example, you destroy a uniquely
valuable book or, in your car, knock down and kill a child, remorse
is merely a side issue. Hebrews indeed says that the apostate cannot
again *repent*. Later it says, 'If we deliberately sin after receiving knowledge of the truth, there can be no further sacrifice for sins' (10:26).
As in the Mosaic Law, there is no forgiveness for deliberate sinning.
'Think how much more severe a penalty will be deserved by anyone
who has trampled underfoot the Son of God, profaned the blood of
the covenant by which he was consecrated, and insulted God's
gracious spirit!' (10:30). To repent means to take the way back. How
can it be possible if that way has been experienced, abandoned and
derided?

As one would expect, this severity (which is compatible with the
treatment of deliberate sinning in Judaism) caused great anxiety in
early centuries of the Church. Today, in countries where the Church
is a struggling community among dominant non-Christian religions,
apostasy would be ruinous of confidence. In our present western
culture, where the Christian religion and Christ himself are commonly
ridiculed in the media and in popular as well as learned publications,
what are we to make of these verses of Hebrews? Anyone who says
'Christianity is all about forgiveness' has entirely failed to see the
problem. We should perhaps ask ourselves whether the Christian life

we offer is, in its own way, as impressive as the life described in Hebrews. Further, if our neighbours are rejecting Christianity – with indifference or contempt – is the fault ours, not theirs? Is our official theology yet adapted for the needs of an actively scientific world, dominated (say) by information technology and genetic engineering? Are the leading persons in our Churches intelligently wise and morally reliable? Should we be expecting apostates to return not by an old path (which of course they cannot) but by helping us to find a new one?

JOHN 8:12–14

> Again Jesus spoke to them, saying, 'I am the light of the world. Whoever follows me will never walk in darkness but will have the light of life.' Then the Pharisees said to him, 'You are testifying on your own behalf; your testimony is not valid.' Jesus answered, 'Even if I testify on my own behalf, my testimony is valid because I know where I have come from and where I am going.' (NRSV)

These verses introduce the third phase of a confrontation between Jesus and the Jewish authorities at the eight-day autumn festival of Tabernacles. 'Tabernacle' is a Latin word meaning tent or movable hut: the reference is to the temporary shelters used during the forty years' wilderness wandering of the Hebrews long ago. By this festival the Jewish people were annually reminded that settled life in town, with trade and farming, was not the only possibility for the people of God. It could even be said that the on-the-move theme was activated by the way that Jesus and his disciples constantly travelled around Galilee and Judaea. But if they were a purposeful wandering group of evangelists they needed instructions. Hence, 'Whoever follows me will never walk in darkness but will have the light of life', that is, they will see what they have to do and how to do it.

There is, of course, more to it than that. 'The light shines in the darkness' (1:5). Jesus shines the light on what is wrong and wicked: for example, the blind, lame and paralysed, one man immobile for thirty-eight years (5:3, 5). 'All who do evil hate the light and do not come to the light, so that their deeds may not be exposed' (3:20). The famous story in chapter 9 of a man born blind who received sight is too often presented solely as the miraculous cure of an optical condition. But the main thrust of the story is towards the miraculous cure of an intractable moral blindness. The Pharisees say, 'Surely we

are not blind, are we?' (9:40). The man says, 'He opened my eyes' –
which all of us may be able to say. Later Jesus says, 'I have come as
light into the world so that everyone who believes in me should not
remain in darkness' (12:46).

It is important to grasp the sense in which the *world* is intended,
for it is a dominant word in this gospel. Indeed John and 1 John
together use the Greek word *kosmos* almost a hundred times, much
more than all the rest of the New Testament. It can mean the great
world in which we live – for the gospel writer, of course, the Mediterranean world. But mostly it means structured human society, which
God loves and intends to save (3:16–17). For that very reason, Jesus
knows where he has come from and where he is going. In a literal
sense (in *this* gospel) Jesus comes and goes a great deal: Galilee,
Judaea, Samaria, beyond the Sea of Galilee, and Transjordan. This is
not an erratic runabout: he knows what he is doing. There is one
simple example: when he hears that Lazarus has died he stays where
he was for two days before going to Bethany. He knows where he is
going because he knows where he has come from, and the Father
'shows him all that he himself is doing' (5:20).

Anyone who now reads John's gospel should not be looking for
answers to ancient historical and theological matters but for a
stimulus to engage with our present personal and social questions.
Perhaps to our surprise and gratitude, our eyes should be opened.
Above all, we should devote consistent energy into asking: Who are
we? Where did we come from? Where are we going? In antiquity
those questions were asked with great seriousness and satisfaction.
So also in many phases of European history. It will not do for us to
give the answer that we are coming from one shopping mall and
going to the next one. Nor should we abandon the Christian religion
when human beings have more power and skill in their hands, for
good or ill, than was conceivable only twenty years ago.

Index